"*You Got This!* will quickly become a classic in your kitchen. Diane creates timeless and nostalgic recipes that still feel creative and fresh. She has a unique ability to make everyday cooking feel special, no matter your occasion or skill level. With so many bookmarked pages already, it's clear that these recipes will be cherished for many years to come!"

—**Carissa Stanton,** *New York Times* bestselling author of *Seriously, So Good*

"In *You Got This!* you'll find a collection of recipes that are as beautiful as they are delicious. . . . [Diane's] debut cookbook makes you feel like you're right there in Mom's kitchen, savoring every bite of food that tastes like a warm hug."

—**Gaby Dalkin,** *New York Times* bestselling author and founder of What's Gaby Cooking

"This cookbook is such a gem! It's full of simple, delicious recipes. . . . Diane's tips make it feel like you've got a personal cheerleader in the kitchen. With this book, you really do got this!"

—**Jennifer Segal, author and founder of Once Upon a Chef**

"Diane is like that awesome family member who always cooks the first thing to disappear on the table. Her recipes are crowd-pleasing, craveable, and always achievable. . . . Pull up a seat at her table—become a part of her family, and become a better cook in the process (and enjoy the process more, too)!"

—**Erin Jeanne McDowell, author of *The Book on Pie* and host of *Happy Baking***

"This cookbook is going to become a staple in my kitchen! My favorite thing about Diane's recipes is that they're not only delicious but also made for real life. I think of her as the people's cook—I always feel like she knows how to hit recipes, methods, and ingredients that so many of us love."

—**Lindsay Ostrom, founder of Pinch of Yum**

"With *You Got This!*, Diane invites us into her kitchen, sharing family stories and the deliciously approachable recipes that have made her a hero to busy home cooks everywhere. Diane's warm and encouraging voice is present on every page, making this book feel immediately accessible to cooks of all levels. *You Got This!* is filled with recipes for the comfort foods we crave, with plenty of veggie-forward updates to fit the way we eat today."

—**Lidey Heuck, author of *Cooking In Real Life***

You Got This!

You Got This!

Recipes Anyone Can Make and Everyone Will Love

Diane Morrisey

Photography by Dane Tashima

SIMON ELEMENT

NEW YORK AMSTERDAM/ANTWERP LONDON TORONTO SYDNEY NEW DELHI

SIMON
ELEMENT

An Imprint of Simon & Schuster, LLC
1230 Avenue of the Americas
New York, NY 10020

First Simon Element hardcover edition March 2025

SIMON ELEMENT is a trademark of Simon & Schuster, LLC

For information about special discounts for bulk purchases,
please contact Simon & Schuster Special Sales at 1-866-506-1949 or
business@simonandschuster.com.

The Simon & Schuster Speakers Bureau can bring authors to your live event. For
more information or to book an event, contact the Simon & Schuster Speakers
Bureau at 1-866-248-3049 or visit our website at www.simonspeakers.com.

Manufactured in China

1 3 5 7 9 10 8 6 4 2

Library of Congress Cataloging-in-Publication Data has been applied for.

ISBN 978-1-6680-3340-1
ISBN 978-1-6680-3341-8 (ebook)

To my mom, Dolores,
who is my biggest inspiration
in every part of my life.

And to my dad, Vito, who was
always my biggest fan.

Breakfast Is My Jam

Almost Dinner

Dinner Time!

Vegetables, Big & Small

Bowls & Salads

Soups & Sammies

Dessert, of Course!

Introduction

Half Gaelic and Half Garlic

I learned from a young age that food is a powerful way to express love and create connection. Most of my childhood memories take place in the kitchen, around our big country-style family table that had an actual church pew on one side. That table was the heart and soul of our house. It's where my siblings and I would unpack the cold cuts and hard rolls from Mom's Saturday grocery haul and make the most killer deli sandwiches. It's where she prepared her legendary cinnamon buns. It's where I watched Grandma's fingers deftly rolling out the pasta dough into gnocchi or cavatelli on her huge wooden board. It's where we hulled strawberries for the jam we made with the pounds of fruit we had just picked.

My mom took her role as a homemaker very seriously. Every afternoon, I would run off the bus, yelling, "Hi, Mom! Did you make anything today?!" And of course, she had. Some days, it was a tray of chocolate chip cookie bars, other times it was frosted chocolate brownies, a pound cake, or, in the summer, a fruit pie. There was *always* something. Every night, the entire family sat down to eat together, and our meal always included a green salad, even if it was just iceberg lettuce with some sliced cucumber and black olives. Mom's food was not fancy. Rather, it was simple, homey, comforting fare, and it's the nourishment that defines my childhood. Mom's cooking—consistent and plentiful—made us feel secure, and that is the feeling I always want to replicate with my own family. Feeding and providing for my family and friends is my daily love letter to them.

Food was there during family celebrations and times of sadness.

I grew up in Monroe, Connecticut, the fourth of six children. My dad was a high school teacher and basketball coach at St. Joseph's High School in Trumbull, one town over. When my brother Andrew began at St. Joe's, Mom took a job in the cafeteria. She said she wanted to get to know our friends. We didn't have a lot of money, but I always felt "rich with family." It's a phrase that my father used. We didn't have much, but we never knew it. Our home was filled with love, laughter, lots and lots of people, and, of course, food. Food was always at the center of everything. It was the great uniter.

Food was there during family celebrations and times of sadness. It *always* brought comfort and prompted us to count our blessings. My parents were first-generation American. My mom's parents came from Belfast, Ireland. Grandma Murphy was not known as a great cook, but she did have her specialties: Irish soda farls (skillet flatbread), boiled turnips, beef stew, and hamburgers fried in a cast-iron skillet with tons of onions. She also had a wicked sweet tooth and always had to have a baked treat to accompany her "wee cuppa." My first forays into baking came when Grandma Murphy asked for something sweet. I'd pick a recipe from one of Mom's cookbooks and bake a simple muffin or a bar cookie. I especially remember a raisin square recipe that she would go gaga over.

My dad's parents came from Bari, Italy, and Grandma Montelli was the most amazing intuitive cook I knew. She made the most memorable meals with a chicken, a few potatoes, and a handful of herbs. Everything she cooked was raised or grown at home, and her gardens were legendary. She is, without a doubt, the biggest influence on my no-fuss cooking philosophy. Her cooking was peasant food: humble, delicious, with lots of big flavors, and budget friendly. That is exactly how I love to cook.

It was an open secret that my mother was *not* my grandmother's first choice for her son's wife. As an only child (and son to boot!) in an Italian family, he was expected to marry an Italian. But my mom eventually weaseled her way into her future mother-in-law's heart by learning how to cook Italian. And with Grandma Montelli's guidance, she mastered my dad's favorite dishes and soon that little blue-eyed Irish lass knew her way around a pot of Sunday sauce (red meat sauce that simmers for hours on the day of rest) better than most.

I studied art in college. Drawing and sketching were my favorite hobbies when I was young and so art school made sense for me. Not long after I graduated, I met my husband, John, at a local beach bar, The Seagrape Café, on the Long Island Sound in Fairfield, Connecticut. During our very first conversation, we bonded over our shared love for our families and how much we adored our nieces and nephews, who were just six months old at the time.

I knew right then that I was going to marry him. I could tell immediately that he was going to be a great father. And I couldn't have been more right.

Our first daughter was born nine months to the day of our wedding and by our tenth anniversary we had six children: three sons and three daughters. With such a busy household, there was no time for art, but I quickly learned that my creativity had a new outlet: the kitchen.

When John and I were married in 1993, I didn't know how to cook. Scrambled eggs and Hamburger Helper were on constant rotation. Hell, I even remember cooking a canned ham! My first dinner party, thrown on the Friday night following our honeymoon, included seven guests: my sisters, MaryAnn and Theresa, and my brother-in-law Frank; my two brothers, Michael and Thomas; and our friends Lauren and Sean. The menu came straight out of *The Silver Palate Cookbook*. I think every bride received a copy at her shower in the 1980s and '90s, along with a stack of books by Martha Stewart, Fannie Farmer, and Better Homes & Gardens. I remember exactly what I made. Dinner that night was creamy chicken and jalapeño nachos, linguine with tomatoes and basil, prosciutto-wrapped shrimp, and strawberry shortcake, John's favorite then and now. Today, this menu would take me a couple of hours from start to finish. But back then, I took the day off work, made a bunch of trips to the store, and spent about twelve hours, with lots of sweating and swearing, and maybe a little crying, getting everything ready. I didn't know what I was doing, but the party was a success.

The birth of the Food Network in 1993 coincided with my marriage and the birth of my first child, Marcelle. A year later, I became a stay-at-home mom, and, as I fell in love with my daughter, I also fell for cooking. I was always trying new recipes, and then inviting people over to have dinner with John and me. The Food Network became my world, and I voraciously read all those cookbooks I had received at my bridal shower. I made weekly excursions, with baby in tow, to the library to peruse more cookbooks, and I started subscribing to food magazines: *Gourmet* and *Bon Appétit* were my favorites. I knew I was supposed to sleep while my newborn slept, but I didn't. Instead, I pored over these cookbooks and magazines.

And that's how I learned to cook. The early Food Network stars—Sara Moulton, Emeril Lagasse, Two Hot Tamales, and David Rosengarten—along with my reading material, were my instructors. I am often asked if I went to culinary school, and I am always proud to reply, "No, I am self-taught." And then I happily add, "And if I can learn on my own, so can you!"

Shortly after I had my third child, I accidentally fell into a catering career. Because John and I were always entertaining, friends began to ask me to help them with their own parties. Slowly but surely, I grew my little business, which also gave me the flexibility to raise my family. I rented a small kitchen near my house, which allowed me to take on more business. Menu planning, catering smaller events, business lunches, and dinner parties kept me busy, but I was also very careful to only take on as much work as I could handle as a mom to six young kids.

During this time, I found myself often driving the forty-five minutes to the Greenwich, Connecticut, Whole Foods to find ingredients that, at the time, I couldn't find at a regular supermarket. The "chef's case" in the prepared foods department was a magnet and revelation. I was in awe of how the platters (grilled vegetables, unusual—for the time—grain and veggie salads, and sliced chicken breast with fruit salsa) were artistically displayed. I used to find so much inspiration in how the platters of colorful and inventive food were designed. It helped me to understand the art of presentation and that garnishes could provide dimension, like crunch, acidity, sweetness, or any other complementary flavor, to my dishes. It was here that I fell in love with the concept of cooking seasonally, because you really do get the best value for your grocery money. I also learned to think out of the cooking box and realized that oftentimes the most creative and beautiful platters of food combined protein, fruit, grains, and greens with an herby aromatic vinaigrette. Cooking boosts creativity through experimentation. Using ingredients in new ways and combining unique flavors and textures will most often yield wonderful and delightful end results!

I loved my excursions to Whole Foods, and a few years later, I accepted what turned out to be my dream job: running their prepared foods departments. Later, I moved into store leadership, where I managed stores in Connecticut and New York City. That store had more than six hundred team members, and, honestly, the skills needed for that job weren't that different from running a large family. I loved working at Whole Foods, and, even more, I loved observing customers' habits. In my years there, I internalized what people gravitate toward: hearty, homey, and comforting foods were the ones that ran out first. At Thanksgiving, my favorite holiday, I would

see people come in and buy ten pounds of mashed potatoes and another ten pounds of stuffing. The cook in me wanted to say "Let me come home with you and teach you how to make these so they are easy and delicious."

And now I can.

My life as a social media influencer started as a happy mistake. One day, I posted on Instagram a birthday cake I had made for one of my children. The picture received more than triple the "likes" of any of my other photos. I posted another of a strawberry pistachio tart, and then a shot of Chicken Divan (page 98), and soon my feed was all food. Slowly but surely, my following grew, and I was pleasantly surprised by how organically it took off. Hell, I barely knew what I was doing. Nevertheless, I have been happily documenting my life as a home cook while I share photos of the real-life recipes I rely on to feed my family of six kids (some grown, but often still at my table) and husband and friends.

The happy accident feels right; I relish the daily DMs and emails from my followers who tell me they are encouraged by my no-nonsense approach to cooking—and that they are inspired either to cook after a lapse, or to start learning how to cook. They remind me that I can show people that cooking can be both uncomplicated and delicious and that it doesn't need to be a stressful chore. I am jazzed beyond belief that I have been able to give people confidence. The same confidence that I drew from all those cookbooks and magazines and TV shows when I was teaching myself.

I'm proud to inspire so many followers, and I am grateful to them for reminding me that we are all dealing with conflicting palates and dietary needs and desires when it comes to menu planning. Vegetarian, gluten-free, lactose intolerant, vegan, nut allergies . . . these dietary restrictions (self-imposed or not) are commonplace. I have been a vegetarian for thirty years, and I remember how friends would shudder at the idea of having to cook something special for me when I was a dinner guest. Those days are over. People are more versatile eaters—and cooks, so accommodating different needs isn't that hard anymore. My trick is to make a vegetarian main course and a simple meat dish to go with it, essentially inverting the plate that I grew up with. For example, if I want to serve my Sweet Potato and Black Bean Enchiladas (page 160), I might grill up Mexican chorizo sausage or a marinated flank steak, too. The vegetarians in the family will take larger portions, while the meat-lovers will use the enchiladas as a side dish. Likewise, Roasted Cauliflower Curry (page 175) can be served with a platter of roasted chicken thighs and legs. Done!

Most cooking isn't perfect, nor should it be.

Cooking is 95 percent confidence and 5 percent the ability to read a recipe. If you trust that you can do it, you will. Just like that first dinner party that took me hours to prepare. The only difference between Diane Then and Diane Now is the confidence that has come with just cooking.

There is another factor that runs throughout my cooking, and my life, which are virtually the same thing. I love cooking because it brings me closer to my family and friends. When we share a meal, we are sharing a common experience. Cooking makes the people I love and the memories of them real for me. Whenever I make Grandma Montelli's braciole (page 125), I think of the wonderful woman who taught me so much about cooking and life. You will see that practically every recipe in this book mentions someone I love. It turns out, I am not alone. When I started posting my recipes for braciole, lasagna, enchiladas, coffee cakes, brownies, and other classic comfort food, they brought back great memories for my followers, too.

Most cooking isn't perfect, nor should it be. You will make mistakes and have some major fails, but there will also be some slam dunks and home runs coming out of your kitchen. You will learn from the bombs and be proud of the successes. That's the process. Most important, though, you will start to relax in the kitchen. And when you do, you will realize, You Got This!

Whether you are single, a parent, a recent graduate, married with no children, or oversee a house full of people, this book will help you up your dinner-time game and enjoy the process and end result. So many people feel intimidated by cooking or think that they don't have the time or ability to make something. This book was written to tell you that you do, that it can be done. Because usually what's missing is not so much time or skill, but belief in yourself. But the more you cook, the more comfortable you will feel doing it and the more confident you will be. And before you know it, preparing wonderful, homey, and memorable meals for your friends and family—and yourself—will be something you enjoy rather than dread.

You Got This! is filled with delicious and beautiful pantry-staple meals that anyone can rely on to feed their family and friends—or just themselves. Some are classics with a twist, and some add a little something to pump them up without adding much extra fuss; other recipes have a little more flair. All of them will make you feel like you got this.

Diane Morrisey

Get Set Up for Success

My food is for real people who need to cook dinner every night. I want this book to inspire you to get into the kitchen, armed with my doable, "honest" recipes. But before that happens, let me help set you up for success. If your pantry is full, and the freezer is stocked, and you have some well-chosen ingredients in the fridge, you are ready to roll! A well-stocked pantry is every good cook's secret weapon. This doesn't have to happen overnight. Allow yourself to gradually build up a kitchen inventory of condiments, seasonings, and basics. Most of these items have long shelf lives and just knowing you have them at hand will assure you that you can cook.

What follows is a list of the kitchen staples that I always keep stocked. I can often make an entire meal from these foods without a last-minute dash to the grocery store.

Pantry

Dried herbs and spices
These add tons of flavor to whatever you are cooking. The ones I most often reach for are **smoked and sweet paprika, ground cumin, chili powder, cayenne, oregano, garlic powder, onion powder, mustard powder**, and **crushed red pepper flakes (chile flakes)**. Use **freshly ground black pepper**, as preground can age and go stale and flavorless. (Of course, in some cases fresh herbs are better; see Refrigerator Staples (page 22) for my faves.)

Fresh garlic and garlic powder
I use tons of garlic. I love fresh garlic, and I have no shame using garlic powder when the moisture in chopped garlic would get in the way, such as spice rubs for meat. When choosing fresh garlic, look for plump, firm heads without any visible green sprouts. Store in a cool place out of direct sunlight, and never in the fridge because the cold and dark environment will encourage sprouting.

Salt
I prefer **kosher salt** for its clean flavor in cooking and the flakiness it adds when used as a finishing salt (sprinkling on food just before serving). There are two major brands: Diamond Crystal in a red box and Morton in a navy blue box. I use Morton, which is most readily available at my market. Weirdly, the two brands are not the same. Diamond's salt crystals are about half the size as Morton's. Therefore, when measuring kosher salt (and in many dishes, I leave seasoning "to taste" up to you), note that ½ teaspoon of Diamond Crystal is the equivalent of 1 teaspoon Morton. If you like to use fine table or sea salt, use the same as Morton, just a little less. A scant teaspoon of fine salt can replace a full teaspoon of Morton kosher.

Canned beans
A can of beans will easily bulk up soups, stews, and salads while adding extra protein. I use **white kidney (cannellini) beans** the most, but **chickpeas, pinto beans**, and **black beans** are good to stock, too.

Bread crumbs
I keep two kinds, **Japanese panko** (with big, crunchy flakes) and the **fine-crumbed Italian-seasoned variety**.

Grains
I rely on grains for added protein. They have a high nutritional value and a long shelf life. **Farro** (Italian wheat berries) is a special favorite for their nutty flavor. I also always have **basmati rice**, **pearl couscous**, **cornmeal**, **old-fashioned (rolled) oats** (good for baking as well as breakfast), and **barley** (great in soups).

Flours
I keep **all-purpose white flour** at room temperature for everyday cooking and baking needs. I store **whole wheat** and **almond flour** in the freezer because they have oils that go rancid at room temperature.

Nuts and seeds
For snacking, baking, salads, and finishing off vegetables with a nice crunch, I am sure to have **almonds**, **cashews**, **pecans**, **walnuts**, and **pumpkin seeds**. They are best when stored in the freezer or fridge.

Pasta and noodles
C'mon! Nothing is better than **dried pasta**. Keep all your faves on hand. For me, that means **rigatoni**, **spaghetti**, **ditalini**, **orzo**, **lasagna**, and **Asian soba** and **rice noodles**.

Crackers
I keep **an assortment** for snacking or dipping with the dips I like to serve as part of the dinner spread.

Canned basics
Crushed tomatoes, diced tomatoes, Italian peeled whole tomatoes in juice, tomato paste, diced green chiles, canned broth (chicken, vegetable, and beef), full-fat (not lite) coconut milk, canned artichokes, marinated artichokes, chipotle peppers in adobo sauce, and **canned tuna.**

Sauces and condiments

Dijon mustard (smooth and grainy), **mayonnaise, ketchup, Thai red curry paste, Calabrian chile paste, gochujang, sweet Thai chili sauce, sriracha, Worcestershire sauce, hot red pepper sauce** (such as Tabasco, and Frank's, which is milder), and **reduced-sodium soy sauce**.

Pickles and preserves

Roasted red peppers, dill pickles (the dill brine is a secret ingredient!), **sweet pickles, pickled jalapeños, pepperoncini**, favorite **jams and preserves, peanut butter, tahini, Mediterranean olives, capers**. Stock flat **anchovy fillets** in oil for the people who like them in salads and on pizza.

Oil and vinegar

Use a moderately priced **extra-virgin olive oil** for both cooking and salads. If you are feeling flush, you could have a pricey boutique extra-virgin olive oil, too, for drizzling on food before serving. **Vegetable, avocado**, and **canola oil** are good because of their neutral flavor. **Toasted sesame oil** has more flavor than the cold-pressed version. Stock a few vinegars, since they all taste a bit different. **Red wine, balsamic, cider**, and **unseasoned rice vinegars** are my go-to's.

Baking staples

For whipping up last-minute treats, I have **dark** and **semisweet** (and **milk** and **white**) **chocolate chips, sweetened coconut flakes, natural cocoa powder, instant espresso powder, brown sugar, granulated sugar, powdered sugar, unsulfured** (mild) **molasses, honey, maple syrup**, and **vanilla extract**.

Refrigerator Staples

Butter   I use **unsalted butter** for cooking, but I also keep **salted butter** on hand for toast.

Cheese   I use cheese a lot in many different ways. For the sandwiches we all love, I stock **sliced American**, **provolone,** and **cheddar**. For casseroles, I always have bags of **shredded cheddar** and **mozzarella**. I keep a **chunk of real Parmigiano-Reggiano** for grating and a **block of Gruyère** for shredding on my box grater. A **log of goat cheese** gets added to many recipes, but I also like to have it for marinating when I need a quick appetizer. I prefer **block feta** to crumbled, but I will use **crumbled Gorgonzola**. **Ricotta** shows up in many of my Italian recipes.

Cured meats   **Prosciutto**, **salami**, and **bacon** keep a long time and bring a lot of flavor to a dish.

Eggs   I use **large eggs**.

Dairy   **Yogurt (plain Greek)** and **sour cream** are long keepers and have many uses in both savory and sweet cooking.

Miso   **White (shiro) miso** is the most versatile.

Fresh herbs   In the summer I plant herbs that will last me until October, but in the colder seasons, I always try to keep **parsley**, **chives**, **oregano**, **basil**, **thyme**, and **cilantro** in the fridge. Extra herbs can be used for chimichurri, Green Goddess dressing, or pesto, and more.

Citrus

Lemons, **limes**, and **oranges** should be in your kitchen for their zest as much as the juice. There is so much flavor in the oils of the zest, it's a shame to throw that out! A good habit is always to zest a lime or lemon before you juice it. Add the zest to bread crumbs or flour before coating meat or fish, add zest to salad dressings, sprinkle on your roasted vegetables for a burst of freshness. For desserts, rub citrus zest into the white sugar with your fingers until it becomes aromatic. Zest-infused sugar will wake up any recipe! You can even freeze the zest the same way I freeze fresh herbs (see How to Freeze Fresh Herbs, below).

Pizza dough

Most stores sell **refrigerated pizza dough** in 1-pound bags. The dough can be turned into strombolis, pizzas, calzones, and other savory baked goods. See more about pizza dough on page 45.

Wine for cooking

I always have **reasonably priced red and white wine** for cooking. The good news is that you don't have to break the bank. Any wine that tastes good to you is going to be great in your cooking. **Pinot Grigio** is a nice choice for a cooking white, and a **Shiraz** works well for a red.

How to Freeze Fresh Herbs

To freeze herbs (sturdy ones, such as rosemary, thyme, and sage work best), sprinkle about 2 tablespoons of chopped herbs into the well of an ice cube tray. Cover with olive oil or water and freeze until solid, about 4 hours or overnight. Pop the cubes out of the tray and transfer to a resealable freezer bag. Use the cubes in dressings, soups, and sauces.

Freezer Staples

Frozen veggies
Some vegetables that are good to have ready when you are include **peas**, **green beans**, **chopped spinach**, and **pearl onions**.

Fruit
I use frozen **peaches**, **mangoes**, and all kinds of **berries** for smoothies and baking.

Shrimp
My freezer always has a bag of **large (21/25 count) peeled and deveined shrimp**. They are incredibly convenient for soups, pastas, and other recipes. Before adding them to a recipe, just thaw in a bowl of cold water for 20 to 30 minutes, drain, and pat dry, and dinner is on the way!

Meats and poultry
Frozen meat and fish can be a lifesaver. Keep a pound or two of **ground beef and/or turkey**, individually wrapped **boneless, skinless chicken breasts**, and some **Italian sausage** in the freezer, and you will be glad you did when you are sure there is nothing to eat for dinner.

Puff pastry
One of my nonnegotiable freezer items for both savory and sweet dishes, **frozen puff pastry** is guaranteed to make you look like a rock star.

Kitchen Tools

A few tools really can make your life easier. I do not have a large kitchen, and so I streamline what's in my toolbelt. I cook for a family of eight and while many people happily use all the available appliances out there (rice cookers, slow cookers, air fryers, electric pressure cookers, and blah-blah-blah), the fact is, I don't have room for them. There is nothing glamorous about the list below, and you may not need each item right away, but over time, you'll be happy you have these few items:

Baking pans and dishes

A standard **half-sheet pan**, measuring 13 × 18 inches, is a must. In fact, you really need a couple, or a few. A **quarter-sheet pan** is about 9 × 13 inches, and I love mine because it is good for smaller amounts of food and fits perfectly into my toaster oven. I have two of them.

I use **9 × 13-inch baking dishes** a lot—metal for baking desserts and bar cookies, and glass ones for savory recipes. Also for baking, I have a **9-inch springform pan**, a **12-cup fluted tube pan (Bundt)**, an **angel food cake pan with a removable bottom**, a **9½-inch pie plate** (because I get a couple of more servings than the smaller 9-inch plate), two **12-cup muffin tins** (why make small batches when muffins freeze so well?), two **8 × 4-inch loaf pans**, one **8-inch square metal baking dish**, and one **9-inch square baking dish**. A **wire cooling rack**, preferably one that fits into a half-sheet pan, is something you might think to pass over, but it does what it is supposed to do perfectly.

Pots and pans

A **large (10- or 12-inch) cast-iron skillet** is great because it holds heat so well and can go from stove to oven. A **large (about 6-quart capacity) enameled Dutch oven** is also indispensable. They have become a lot more affordable over the years. A **large (12- to 14-inch) sauté pan with straight sides** is good for searing. You want a wide cooking surface because if the food is crowded, it will steam, and not brown. For other uses, such as eggs at breakfast time, a **medium (10-inch) nonstick skillet** is very handy. I also have a **large stockpot (about 12 quarts)** for when I am *really* cooking up a lot of food.

Miscellaneous tools

Immersion blender (for soups and sauces), **kitchen shears, tongs, box grater, bench scraper, Microplane zester** (for grating citrus zest and hard cheese), a few different **flexible silicone or rubber spatulas, wooden spoons, slotted spoon, instant-read thermometer, olive oil cruet with pourer, citrus juicer, fine-mesh sieve, parchment paper, heavy-duty blender, electric hand mixer,** and **whisks** (various sizes).

Chicken Parmesan
with Vodka Sauce (page 132)

What I Was Thinking When I Wrote This Book

I want you to break out of the dinner rut. I have organized the dishes by mood more than ingredients. Listing recipes by poultry, red meat, seafood, desserts, and so on can be useful, but it's not the way I fly. Sometimes I take a buffet or smorgasbord approach to the meal and put out an array of food that some might consider snacks. (This is also a great way to put out leftovers.) And sometimes we all need a fancy-ish menu for guests; other times finger food is just fine . . . and fun to eat. The vegetarians and omnivores in my family coexist in harmony because I have lots of satisfying vegetable dishes (including "bowls") that everyone loves—or I bolster the vegetable one with grilled chicken or sliced steak or sautéed shrimp.

Within some chapters, you will notice that I've grouped recipes together into categories that are outside of the box. For example, I've collected three recipes for galettes (a free-form French tart) with three variations on a basic dough (page 64). I also show you a few ways to use pizza dough (pages 71 to 74) beyond its original use.

So let these recipes and words inspire you to cook and crank you up until you shout out, "I got this!"

Breakfast Is My Jam

I am the kind of person who can happily eat

breakfast morning, noon, and night. Maybe that's why I love to make savory breakfasts (frittatas) as much as sweet ones (pancakes and French toast). I go to bed thinking about what I will be eating in the morning, and I have been known to go to bed earlier just so breakfast will come sooner.

For many people, weekday breakfast means gulping a fistful of cereal, a piece of fruit, or a granola bar while running out the door, but you'd be surprised how many opportunities there are with just a little planning or smart use of leftovers to make a good breakfast Monday through Friday. And, if you're the type who would rather sleep an extra thirty minutes instead of making breakfast, I offer plenty of scrumptious recipes for weekend cooking when you have a bit more time. And! when you want something fancy for a special breakfast or brunch, I've provided a trio of hot-from-the-oven treats based on store-bought doughs. It's all about planning ahead and stocking the pantry, fridge, and freezer so that you are good to go, even while you are sipping that first cup of coffee or tea.

French Toast Sticks with Two Sauces

Strawberry Compote

12 ounces strawberries, hulled and halved, or about 2 cups blueberries or raspberries

1/4 cup sugar

1 tablespoon fresh lemon juice

2 teaspoons cornstarch

Maple Butter Sauce

1/2 cup pure maple syrup

4 tablespoons unsalted butter, cut up

French Toast Sticks

5 slices sweet sandwich bread, such as brioche loaf, Texas toast, or challah, preferably day-old

3 large eggs

1/4 cup whole milk

Pinch of kosher salt

1/2 cup sugar

1½ teaspoons ground cinnamon

3 tablespoons unsalted butter, plus more as needed

SERVES 4 TO 6 I made these all the time when my kids were small because they positively loved them, but truth be told, I love them just as much as they do. In fact, I've been known to dream about these. These are more than your average French toast.

1. **MAKE THE STRAWBERRY COMPOTE:** In a medium saucepan, combine the strawberries, sugar, and lemon juice and mash the berries with a fork to release some juices. Bring to a simmer over medium heat. Reduce the heat to medium-low and simmer, stirring often, until the mixture is juicy, about 5 minutes.

2. In a small bowl, whisk the cornstarch into 1/4 cup water. Stir into the strawberry mixture, return to a simmer, and cook, mashing often with the fork to break up the berries, until the compote has lightly thickened, about 5 minutes. Transfer to a bowl and let cool until tepid.

3. **MAKE THE MAPLE BUTTER SAUCE:** Heat the maple syrup and butter in a small saucepan over medium heat, whisking often, until the butter melts and the mixture is combined. Transfer to a bowl and let cool until tepid.

4. Preheat the oven to 200°F.

5. **MAKE THE FRENCH TOAST STICKS:** Cut each bread slice into strips about 1 inch wide. In a medium bowl, whisk the eggs, milk, and salt. In a shallow baking dish, whisk the sugar and cinnamon to combine.

6. Melt the butter in a large skillet over medium heat. Working in batches to avoid crowding the strips, add the bread to the egg mixture and roll quickly to coat without soaking them. Add to the skillet and cook, turning once, until golden brown on both sides, about 3 minutes. Transfer to a heatproof platter and keep warm in the oven. Repeat with the remaining bread and custard, adding more butter to the skillet as needed.

7. In batches, toss the warm French toast strips in the cinnamon sugar and return to the platter. Serve warm with the compote and maple butter sauce for dipping.

Chard, Potato, and Red Pepper Frittata

5 ounces Swiss chard (about ½ bunch), washed very well (or other leafy greens)

4 tablespoons olive oil

1 pound red-skinned potatoes, scrubbed but unpeeled, cut into medium dice

1 yellow onion, chopped

1 garlic clove, finely chopped

½ cup chopped drained jarred roasted peppers

½ teaspoon smoked paprika

¼ teaspoon cayenne pepper

1 teaspoon kosher salt

¼ teaspoon freshly ground black pepper

8 large eggs

¼ cup whole milk or heavy cream

¼ cup freshly grated Parmigiano-Reggiano cheese

¼ teaspoon crushed red pepper flakes

SERVES 6 TO 8 I call frittatas my "weekend heroes" because if I don't have all the ingredients below, I just throw together 2 cups of chopped cooked vegetables left over from the previous week. They are great morning fare, but don't neglect them for lunch or a light dinner. And leftover frittatas make great sandwiches with tomatoes and spicy mayo. I bake frittatas in a cast-iron skillet because it conducts the heat very well for even cooking, and it can safely go from stovetop to oven to table. Other greens can stand in for the Swiss chard if you wish. Try escarole, spinach, collard or dandelion greens, frisée, or arugula. You can also add some cooked bacon or browned prosciutto to the frittata.

1. Strip the chard leaves from the stems and cut the stems crosswise into ½-inch lengths. Stack the leaves and cut them into 1-inch-wide strips, then coarsely chop them. Keep the stems and leaves separate.

2. Preheat the oven to 350°F. Heat 1 tablespoon of the oil in a 10- to 12-inch heavy ovenproof skillet (preferably cast-iron) over medium heat. Add the chard stems, cover, and cook, stirring occasionally, until the stems begin to soften, about 4 minutes. In batches, stir in the chard leaves and cover, letting the first batch wilt before adding more. When all the chard has been added, cover and cook, stirring occasionally, until tender, about 5 minutes. Transfer to a bowl.

3. Wipe out the skillet. Add the remaining 3 tablespoons of oil and heat over medium heat. Add the potatoes and onion, cover, and cook, stirring occasionally, until they are tender but not browned, about 15 minutes.

4. Move the potatoes over to make an empty space in the skillet. Add the garlic to the empty space and cook until fragrant, about 1 minute. Pour off any liquid from the chard and scatter the chard into the skillet. Add the roasted peppers, smoked paprika, cayenne, salt, and black pepper and mix well.

Continues

5. In a large bowl, whisk together the eggs, milk, Parmigiano, and pepper flakes. Pour over the vegetables in the skillet and shake the pan to distribute the eggs.

6. Cook, without stirring, until the eggs are bubbling up and set around the edges, 3 to 5 minutes.

7. Transfer to the oven and bake until the frittata is puffed, lightly browned, and the top feels set when pressed in the center, 25 to 30 minutes.

8. Remove from the oven and let stand for 10 minutes before serving.

Avocado and Bacon Sandwiches with Sheet Pan Eggs

Olive oil

12 large eggs

Kosher salt and freshly ground black pepper

Finely chopped fresh chives, for sprinkling

8 slices whole wheat bread, toasted

½ cup Romesco (page 58), Muhammara (page 76), or store-bought red pepper hummus

2 Hass avocados, halved lengthwise and sliced

6 bacon slices, cooked, cut in half to make 12 pieces

8 tomato slices

MAKES 4 SANDWICHES Don't think you have enough time to fry up a bunch of eggs in the morning? Think again. If you're cooking for a crowd, these are a terrific way to make eggs for breakfast sandwiches.

Preheat the oven and sheet pan, drizzle with olive oil, drop on the eggs, and bake away! So much easier than frying, egg-by-egg! A half-sheet pan will hold a full dozen eggs. For 6 eggs, I use my toaster oven sheet pan (aka, a quarter-sheet pan). There is one important tip to know here: Fresher eggs hold their shape better than ones that have been around for more than a week, as the latter tend to spread and run in the pan.

1. Preheat the oven to 425°F. Heat a half-sheet pan in the oven at the same time, about 15 minutes.

2. When the oven reaches temperature, remove the pan from the oven and drizzle it generously with oil, tilting the pan to be sure it is entirely coated. Crack the eggs onto the sheet. Return the sheet pan to the oven and bake until the eggs are set and no longer jiggle when the pan is shaken and the yolks are set but still runny, about 12 minutes.

3. Remove from the oven and season with salt and pepper and sprinkle with chives.

4. For each sandwich, spread 2 slices of toast with about 2 tablespoons of the romesco. Fan out an avocado half on one of the slices, season with salt and pepper, and top with 3 bacon half-slices. Using a pancake turner, cut the fried eggs into 4 portions with 3 yolks per portion (they don't have to be perfect) and transfer a portion to the sandwich. Add 2 tomato slices. Cap with the other bread slice, spread-side down, and cut in half. Serve immediately.

Egg Clouds in Ciabatta Boats

4 ciabatta rolls

4 large eggs

½ teaspoon hot sauce, such as Tabasco

¼ teaspoon kosher salt

Pinch of freshly ground black pepper

½ cup shredded mozzarella cheese

4 bacon slices, cooked and crumbled

Finely chopped fresh chives, for garnish

SERVES 4 Egg clouds are perfect for an impressive breakfast or brunch. And they are ridiculously easy to make. You start with store-bought rolls and then whip the egg whites and slip them into crusty bread shells to bake into fluffy "clouds." After a few minutes in the oven, add the yolks to the toasty "boats," and in a few minutes, you'll end up with a "sun" poking through. For a vegetarian meal, just leave out the bacon or top with your favorite roasted vegetables—zucchini, peppers, or onions.

1. Preheat the oven to 400°F. Line a half-sheet pan with parchment paper.

2. Cut off the top dome from each roll, about ½ inch from the top. Then pull out the crumb from each roll to make a boat with a ½-inch-thick border. (Save the "lids" and pulled-out crumbs for another use, such as making bread crumbs.) Place the ciabatta boats on the half-sheet pan.

3. Separate the eggs, putting the whites into a medium bowl and carefully placing the yolks into a small bowl, being sure not to break the yolks.

4. With an electric mixer, whip the egg whites just until they form soft peaks. Add the hot sauce, salt, and pepper and whip more until stiff peaks form. Carefully fold in the mozzarella—you don't want to deflate the whites. Divide the mixture evenly among the ciabatta boats. Using the back of a spoon, make an indentation in the center of each "cloud" to hold the yolks later.

5. Bake until the whites are partially set and beginning to brown, 6 to 8 minutes. Remove the half-sheet pan with the ciabatta boats from the oven. Use a soup spoon to carefully slip a yolk into each indentation in the whites. Return to the oven and bake until the yolks and whites are set, 6 to 8 minutes, for runny yolks. For firmer yolks, bake a few minutes longer.

6. Place each boat on a dinner plate. Sprinkle with the bacon and chives and serve hot.

Lemon Ricotta Pancakes with Blueberry Compote

Blueberry Compote

2 cups blueberries, fresh or frozen

3 tablespoons sugar

2 tablespoons fresh lemon juice

1½ teaspoons cornstarch

Pancakes

1½ cups all-purpose flour

3 tablespoons sugar

2 teaspoons baking powder

¼ teaspoon baking soda

½ teaspoon kosher salt

1 cup whole milk

¾ cup ricotta cheese, whole-milk or part-skim

3 large eggs, lightly beaten

1 teaspoon vanilla extract

Finely grated zest of 1 lemon

¼ cup fresh lemon juice

Melted butter, for the griddle

SERVES 4 TO 6 Pancakes just make me so happy—and I know I'm not alone. These ricotta pancakes are super soft, fluffy, and bursting with flavor. The ricotta adds a lightness while the lemon gives it a bit of a tangy flavor that you are going to love. And the sweetness from the blueberry compote is the perfect accompaniment, making these quite the brunch showstopper.

1. **MAKE THE BLUEBERRY COMPOTE:** In a medium saucepan, combine the blueberries, sugar, and lemon juice. Bring to a simmer over medium heat, stirring often to dissolve the sugar. In a small custard cup or ramekin, sprinkle the cornstarch over 2 tablespoons of water and stir to dissolve. Stir the cornstarch mixture into the blueberry mixture and bring to a simmer. Reduce the heat to low and simmer, stirring often, until the juices thicken, about 2 minutes. Remove from the heat and let cool until tepid.

2. **MAKE THE PANCAKES:** In a medium bowl, whisk together the flour, sugar, baking powder, baking soda, and salt. In a separate bowl, whisk the milk, ricotta, eggs, vanilla, lemon zest, and lemon juice—it may look curdled, but don't worry about it. It's fine. Make a well in the center of the dry ingredients, pour in the wet ingredients, and mix just until combined (it will be slightly lumpy).

3. Preheat the oven to 200°F. Heat a large nonstick griddle or skillet over medium-high heat. Brush the skillet with some melted butter. Using ⅓ cup batter for each, portion the batter onto the skillet. Cook until the undersides are golden, about 2 minutes. Flip the pancakes to cook the other sides, about 2 minutes more. To keep warm before serving, transfer the pancakes directly to the oven rack (without a half-sheet pan). Continue with the remaining batter.

4. Serve the hot pancakes with the warm compote.

Ham, Cheese, and Chive Muffins

Cooking spray

2 cups all-purpose flour

1 tablespoon sugar

2½ teaspoons baking powder

1 teaspoon garlic powder

½ teaspoon baking soda

¼ teaspoon kosher salt

¼ rounded teaspoon smoked paprika

1 cup buttermilk

4 tablespoons unsalted butter, melted

1 large egg, lightly beaten

1 tablespoon Dijon mustard

1½ cups chopped Gruyère cheese

1 cup chopped ham

¼ cup finely chopped fresh chives or 1 scallion, white and green parts, finely chopped

MAKES 18 REGULAR OR 6 JUMBO MUFFINS These muffins are the perfect thing to make if you have leftover holiday ham. Swap out the Gruyère for another semihard cheese (like cheddar, Cantal, or fontina) if you wish. These are wonderful hot out of the oven at breakfast, split in half and with a fried egg sandwiched in the middle. But at other meals, serve these hearty muffins with butter as sidekicks to soup or salad or when you want a savory addition to the table breadbasket. I always make a full batch of these because they freeze like a dream. You will need 18 muffin cups (one 12-cup and one 6-cup pan) for these or use a single pan and bake in batches. Another option is to portion the batter into a 6-cup jumbo muffin tin and bake them for a few minutes longer.

1. Preheat the oven to 375°F. Line 18 standard muffin cups or one 6-cup jumbo muffin tin with paper liners. (If you are not using a nonstick pan, mist the exposed metal on the top of the pan with cooking spray so the muffin tops come out easily.)

2. In a medium bowl, whisk together the flour, sugar, baking powder, garlic powder, baking soda, salt, and smoked paprika. In a separate bowl, whisk together the buttermilk, melted butter, egg, and mustard. Make a well in the center of the dry ingredients, pour in the wet ingredients, and stir just until barely combined—it should be a little lumpy. Add the Gruyère, ham, and chives and fold them in. Do not overmix. Divide the batter evenly among the cups.

3. Bake until the muffins are golden and a toothpick inserted in the center comes out clean, about 25 minutes for the standard muffins or about 30 minutes for the jumbo muffins.

4. Let cool in the pan for 5 minutes, then remove from the cups. Serve warm. (Cooled muffins can be frozen in a freezer storage bag for up to 2 months. Microwave on high in 15-second increments for about 45 seconds, or until thawed and warm.)

Breakfast Calzones

Olive oil, for the sheet pan and brushing

1 pound refrigerated pizza dough, at room temperature (see Note)

All-purpose flour, for dusting

4 large eggs

¼ teaspoon kosher salt

⅛ teaspoon freshly ground black pepper

1 tablespoon olive oil

1 cup cheese: shredded cheddar, Swiss, fontina, Monterey Jack, pepper Jack, provolone, or mozzarella; herbed cheese spread (such as Boursin); crumbled goat cheese, or a combination

½ cup chopped cooked meat: bacon, breakfast or Italian sausage, ham, pancetta, soft or hard chorizo, or a combination

Everything bagel seasoning, for topping

Marinara Sauce (page 126), Pico de Gallo (page 61), or Avocado Lime Crema (page 162), for serving

MAKES 2 LARGE CALZONES (SERVES 4 TO 6) Breakfast calzones are a great way to start a weekend morning. Take a peek in the fridge, and you will see all sorts of staples and leftover ingredients to add to a base of scrambled eggs. Grown-ups and kids alike enjoy choosing their favorite fillings from meats to vegetables, always held together with some cheese. While these calzones are filled with one of my favorite cheese-and-breakfast-meat combinations, you will easily come up with your own preferred filling. Usually, I make one meaty calzone and the second as a veggie option. (See the vegetable variations that follow.) Be sure to allow time for the dough to come to room temperature.

1. Preheat the oven to 400°F. Lightly oil a half-sheet pan (two calzones will both fit on the pan).

2. Cut the dough in half and shape each portion into a ball. Place on a lightly floured work surface, cover with a damp kitchen towel, and let stand while preparing the fillings.

3. In a small bowl, beat the eggs and season with a pinch each of salt and pepper. Heat the oil in a small nonstick skillet over medium heat. Add the eggs and cook, stirring almost constantly, until the eggs are barely set and still somewhat wet, about 1 minute. (They are going to bake again in the oven, so you want them undercooked at this stage.) Transfer the eggs to a bowl to cool slightly (don't leave in the skillet or they will keep cooking).

4. On a lightly floured work surface, roll out one dough ball into a 12-inch round. (If the dough springs back, cover the partially rolled round with the towel, let it relax and warm up at room temperature for 5 to 10 minutes, then try again.) Transfer the dough to one side of the half-sheet pan (after this calzone is folded, you want room on the pan for the second calzone).

5. On the bottom half of the round, sprinkle half of the cheese, followed by half of the cooked eggs and half of the meat. Brush the edge of the round with water and fold in half. Press the edges together well, then tightly pinch and crimp the dough around the edge to seal. Cut 2 slits in the top of the calzone, brush with oil, and sprinkle with the bagel seasoning. Repeat with the remaining dough and fillings, moving the calzones so they both fit on the pan.

6. Bake until golden brown, 15 to 20 minutes.

7. Cut the calzones still on the half-sheet pan into serving portions and serve hot from the pan, with the sauce of your choice on the side.

VARIATIONS

Vegetable Calzones: Omit the meat. For each calzone, use ½ cup cooked and chopped vegetables, such as red or green bell peppers, spinach or other greens, eggplant, caramelized or regular onions, broccoli florets, or mushrooms, or a combination. Use ½ cup cheese for each calzone.

Potato Calzones: Omit the meat. For each calzone, use ½ cup chopped cooked (boiled, baked, or fried) potatoes, Tater Tots, or hash browns. Use ½ cup cheese for each calzone.

Frittata Calzones: Instead of the scrambled eggs, substitute ½ cup chopped frittata (any flavor). Use ½ cup cheese for each calzone.

Working with Refrigerated Pizza Dough

Pizza dough, sold in a plastic bag in the supermarket's refrigerated section, is a boon to the busy home cook. There is one little catch. When the dough is cold, it is a pain to roll out . . . and this can drive you crazy. The dough needs to be room temperature for it to stretch and roll properly without retracting. But you need to allow time for the dough to warm up in a warm place for 45 minutes to 1½ hours. But what is a warm place? The desired temperature is about 80°F. One reliable location is an oven (standard or microwave) with an interior light. Leave the door ajar, and the bulb will radiate enough heat to help warm the dough.

You can also *gently* microwave the dough. You don't want it to cook, just warm up. Microwave the dough at low power (20 to 30 percent) in 15-second increments, flipping the dough over after each session, until you can feel that the dough surface is no longer cold, about 1½ minutes. Be flexible with the timing to allow for the power differences in microwave ovens. Let the dough stand for 5 to 10 minutes at room temperature after microwaving to distribute the warmth through the dough.

Chocolate Streusel Coffee Cake

Cooking spray

6 ounces (1 cup) semisweet chocolate chips

½ cup sweetened coconut flakes

½ cup coarsely chopped walnuts

½ cup sugar

1 teaspoon ground cinnamon

1 15.25-ounce box yellow cake mix

1 3.4-ounce package instant vanilla pudding

1 cup sour cream

4 large eggs

½ cup canola or vegetable oil

1 teaspoon vanilla extract

SERVES 12 My mom made this beautiful, old-fashioned cinnamon coffee cake every Christmas morning. I've carried on the tradition of serving this cake to my own family as we open gifts, and I'd like to think that my children will do the same with their families as well. Even on the busiest morning of the year, this recipe is super simple with a cake and pudding mix hack. This is my brother Michael's favorite cake and he is sure to drop by every Christmas morning to get a slice of it . . . and some nostalgia on the side.

1. Preheat the oven to 350°F. Coat the inside of a tube pan with a removable bottom (aka angel food cake pan) with the cooking spray.

2. In a medium bowl, mix together the chocolate chips, coconut, walnuts, sugar, and cinnamon.

3. In a large bowl with an electric mixer, beat the cake mix, pudding mix, sour cream, eggs, oil, and vanilla on medium speed, scraping down the sides of the bowl as needed, for 2 minutes.

4. Scrape half of the batter into the pan. Top with half of the chocolate chip mixture. Cover with the remaining batter and smooth the top. Sprinkle with the remaining chocolate chip mixture.

5. Bake until a wooden skewer inserted in the center of the cake comes out clean (don't touch the hot chocolate chips!), 50 minutes to 1 hour.

6. Let cool completely in the pan on a wire rack.

7. Run a knife around the inside of the cake pan and the tube to release the cake. Lift up on the bottom insert to unmold the cake. Cut the cake along the bottom of the insert to release it and lift up the cake to transfer to a serving plate. Slice and serve.

Smoked Turkey Croissant Roll-Ups

1 tablespoon unsalted butter

4 large eggs

½ teaspoon kosher salt

¼ teaspoon freshly ground black pepper

1 scallion, white and green parts, thinly sliced

1 8-ounce tube refrigerated crescent roll dough, such as Pillsbury

All-purpose flour, for rolling

4 teaspoons Dijon mustard

4 ounces thinly sliced smoked turkey or ham

1 cup packed baby spinach

1 cup shredded Gruyère or Swiss cheese

Egg wash: 1 large egg beaten with 1 teaspoon water

Everything bagel seasoning, for sprinkling

MAKES 4 ROLL-UPS With a tube of refrigerated crescent roll dough, I can work some serious magic at breakfast time. Here is a mash-up of a ham and cheese croissant and an American breakfast sandwich. I love this with warmed raspberry jam. In a few minutes, you will have a breakfast treat that will keep everyone satisfied at least until lunch.

1. Preheat the oven to 375°F. Melt the butter in a medium nonstick skillet over medium heat. In a medium bowl, whisk together the eggs, salt, and pepper and pour into the skillet. Cook, stirring often, just until the eggs are barely set (they should remain shiny and a bit undercooked), about 1 minute. Stir in the scallion. Remove from the heat and let cool while preparing the rolls.

2. Open the dough and unroll onto a lightly floured work surface. Press the perforated cuts in the dough together to close the seams. Using a pizza cutter or a large knife, cut the dough in half crosswise and then lengthwise to make 4 equal rectangles.

3. For each roll, spread 1 teaspoon of the mustard over the dough rectangle. Place one-quarter of the turkey on top, followed by one-quarter of the spinach. Sprinkle with ¼ cup of the cheese, then one-quarter of the eggs. Starting at a short end, roll up each into a cylinder and place on the half-sheet pan, seam-side down. Brush with the egg wash and sprinkle with the bagel seasoning.

4. Bake until golden brown, about 15 minutes. Serve hot.

Mushroom and Prosciutto Tart

Tart Shell

All-purpose flour, for rolling

Half a 17.3-ounce package (1 sheet) frozen puff pastry, thawed

Egg wash: 1 large egg beaten with 1 teaspoon water

2 tablespoons Dijon mustard

Filling

1 tablespoon olive oil

6 thin slices prosciutto

2 teaspoons unsalted butter

10 cremini mushrooms, thinly sliced

1 cup shredded sharp cheddar cheese

¼ cup plain Greek low-fat yogurt

2 tablespoons freshly grated Parmigiano-Reggiano cheese

2 large eggs, lightly beaten

2 garlic cloves, finely chopped

2 tablespoons finely chopped fresh chives

1 teaspoon chopped fresh thyme

1 teaspoon kosher salt

¼ teaspoon freshly ground black pepper

SERVES 6 TO 8 This lovely savory tart can be eaten for breakfast, brunch, lunch, or dinner. Or just slice it up into bite-sized pieces and enjoy it with a cocktail. And while I use mushrooms and prosciutto, it can also be made with other cooked veggies (I'm thinking asparagus, broccoli, or zucchini).

1. **BAKE THE TART SHELL:** Preheat the oven to 400°F. Line a half-sheet pan with parchment paper.

2. On a lightly floured work surface, gently roll the pastry into an 11-inch square. Transfer to the prepared half-sheet pan. Using a small sharp knife, score a 1-inch border around the edges of the square, like a frame, taking care not to cut through the pastry. Using a fork, thoroughly pierce the pastry in the center area inside the "frame." Brush the border with the egg wash.

3. Bake until golden, 12 to 15 minutes. Remove from the oven but leave the oven on.

4. Press down any puffed area inside of the pastry frame with the back of the fork, leaving the border intact. Spread the mustard over the inside of the frame.

5. **MAKE THE FILLING:** Heat the oil in a large skillet over medium-high heat. In batches, if necessary, add the prosciutto and cook, turning once, until curled and crispy, about 4 minutes. Transfer to paper towels to drain and cool. Crumble the prosciutto.

6. Add the butter to the skillet and melt. Add the mushrooms and cook, stirring occasionally, until the juices have evaporated and the mushrooms are lightly browned, about 8 minutes. Transfer to a bowl.

7. Scatter the mushrooms and prosciutto over the mustard in the center of the pastry. In a medium bowl, whisk together the yogurt, Parmigiano, eggs, garlic, chives, thyme, salt, and pepper. Pour over the vegetables, letting the pastry frame contain the filling.

8. Return the tart to the oven and bake until the filling is set, 12 to 15 minutes.

9. Let cool for a few minutes in the pan. Transfer to a serving platter, slice, and serve.

Blueberry Turnovers

Filling

2 cups blueberries, fresh or frozen

½ cup sugar

1 tablespoon cornstarch

Grated zest of 1 lemon

1 teaspoon fresh lemon juice

Turnovers

All-purpose flour for rolling the pastry

1 17.3-ounce package (2 sheets) frozen puff pastry, thawed

Egg wash: 1 large egg beaten with 1 teaspoon water

MAKES 8 TURNOVERS These super-simple blueberry turnovers make the perfect grab-and-go breakfast, quick snack, or, with the addition of ice cream, a delicious dessert in a bowl. Any berry can be switched out for the blueberries (hull and slice strawberries first). Turnovers are also perfect for entertaining because they can be assembled ahead of time, and then covered and parked in the fridge until you are ready to bake them off.

1. **MAKE THE FILLING:** In a small saucepan, toss the berries with the sugar. Cook over medium heat, stirring occasionally, until the berries give off their juices, about 5 minutes. In a small bowl, add 1 tablespoon water, sprinkle in the cornstarch, and stir to dissolve. Stir into the blueberry mixture with the lemon zest and juice. Reduce the heat to low and simmer, stirring often, until thickened, about 10 minutes. Transfer to a medium bowl and let cool completely. (The filling can be covered and refrigerated for up to 2 days.)

2. **ASSEMBLE THE TURNOVERS:** Preheat the oven to 400°F. Line a half-sheet pan with parchment paper.

3. On a lightly floured work surface, roll out one sheet of the puff pastry into a 12-inch square. Cut crosswise in half, and then lengthwise in half to make four 6-inch squares. Spoon one-eighth of the cooled filling in the center of a square. Brush the egg wash around the edges of the square. Fold in half, top right corner to bottom left corner, to make a triangle. Using the tines of a fork, press and seal the edges. Transfer to the half-sheet pan. Repeat with the remaining pastry and filling to make 8 turnovers. (The turnovers can be covered with plastic wrap and refrigerated for up to 1 day.)

4. Using a small knife, cut 2 small slashes on top of each turnover. Lightly brush the tops of the turnovers with the egg wash.

5. Bake until puffed and golden brown, about 20 minutes.

6. Cool slightly and serve warm or cooled to room temperature.

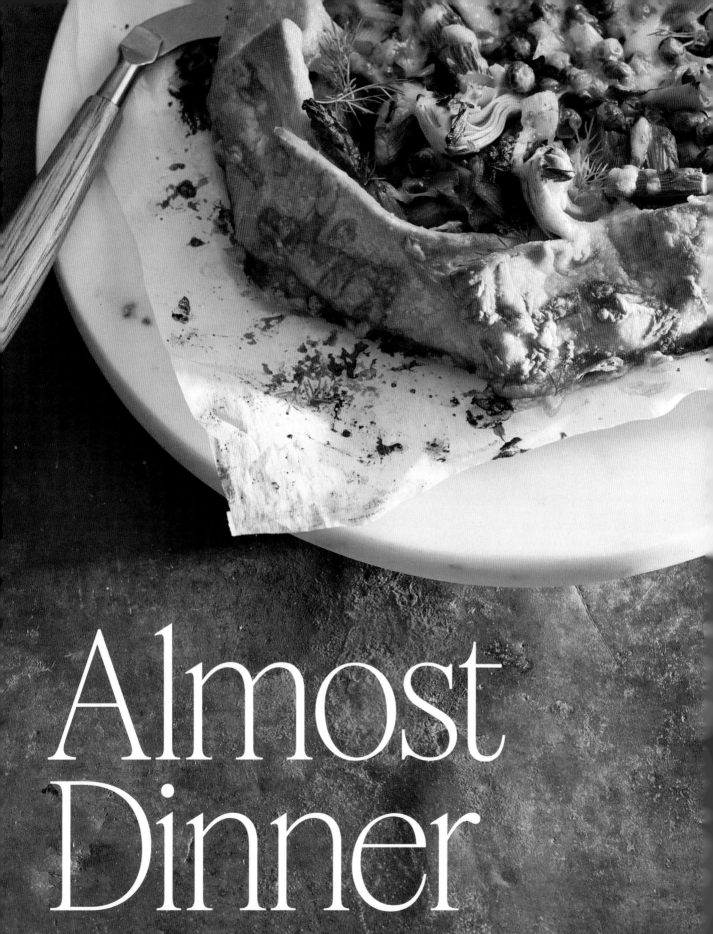

Almost
Dinner

Dinner can be whatever you want it to be.

Too often, when we are looking for dinner inspiration, we get stuck in the mentality that the menu must consist of a main dish with a few additional dishes, whether a vegetable, grain, or another thing on the side, to be a complete meal.

At our house, I often opt for a less traditional approach. I've collected casual recipes, the sort you might think of as party hors d'oeuvres and snacks, into a few loose categories: fritters; galettes (free-form savory pies that are amazingly versatile); ideas for store-bought pizza dough beyond its typical use; and things you can make with puff pastry (a supermarket staple I use as a foundation for savory recipes).

I offer a collection of my gang's favorite dips, and I round out my list of "recipes formerly known as appetizers" with some crispy morsels from the oven. These recipes take off the nightly "dinner pressure." Serve a couple of these easy dishes with a simple salad and have some fun playing with the very idea of what dinner can be.

Garbanzo Bean and Sun-Dried Tomato Fritters with Romesco

1 15-ounce can garbanzo beans (chickpeas), drained and rinsed

3 scallions, white and green parts, thinly sliced

1/3 cup finely chopped oil-packed sun-dried tomatoes, drained

1/4 cup all-purpose flour, plus more for shaping the fritters

1 large egg, lightly beaten

1/4 cup finely chopped fresh basil

1/4 cup freshly grated Parmigiano-Reggiano cheese

1/4 cup panko bread crumbs

1 teaspoon ground cumin

1/2 teaspoon garlic powder

1/2 teaspoon kosher salt

1/4 teaspoon freshly ground black pepper

Vegetable oil, for shallow-frying

Romesco (recipe follows), for serving

SERVES 8 Garbanzo beans (aka chickpeas) are full of protein, fiber, vitamins, and minerals and I use them in many recipes, from main courses to salads. These fritters are economical, easy, and very versatile. I've served them on greens, with a side of roasted sweet potato wedges, as a sandwich in pita, or bite-sized as an appetizer with romesco for dipping. Don't skimp on the romesco, which would make a rubber tire taste delectable.

1. In a large bowl crush the garbanzo beans with a potato masher or fork until the beans are almost smooth. Add the scallions, sun-dried tomatoes, flour, egg, basil, Parmigiano, panko, cumin, garlic powder, salt, and pepper and mix well. Let stand until the batter firms up slightly, about 15 minutes.

2. Line a half-sheet pan with paper towels and place near the stove. Pour 1/2 inch of oil into a large skillet. Heat over medium-high heat until the oil is shimmering.

3. Using floured hands, shape the batter into 8 patties about 1/2 inch thick. Slip the patties into the oil, taking care not to splash the oil. Fry until the underside is golden, about 3 minutes. Flip the fritters and fry the other sides until golden, about 3 minutes more. Using a slotted spatula, transfer to the paper towels to drain briefly.

4. Serve hot with the romesco.

Continues

ROMESCO

Makes about 3 cups

3/4 cup sliced almonds, natural or blanched

3 garlic cloves, smashed and peeled

1 12-ounce jar roasted red peppers, drained and patted dry

1/2 cup coarsely chopped oil-packed sun-dried tomatoes, drained

1/4 cup finely chopped fresh parsley

1 tablespoon fresh lemon juice

1 tablespoon red wine vinegar

1 teaspoon smoked paprika

Freshly grated zest of 1/2 lemon

1/2 teaspoon cayenne pepper

1/3 cup extra-virgin olive oil

Kosher salt

This Spanish sauce is smoky, slightly sweet, and bursting with flavor. You'll be glad you made a large batch because it is a terrific dip and sandwich spread, or serve it as a condiment for grilled chicken, steaks, chops, or veggies. It can also be tossed with pasta or spread on a crostini. However you enjoy it, it's going to take the dish up a notch.

1. In a food processor, process the almonds and garlic together until they are the consistency of coarse cornmeal. Add the roasted red peppers, sun-dried tomatoes, parsley, lemon juice, vinegar, smoked paprika, lemon zest, and cayenne and process until very finely chopped.

2. With the machine running, gradually pour in the oil and process until combined. Season with salt.

3. Transfer to a serving bowl. Let stand for about 30 minutes to blend the flavors. (The romesco can be transferred to a covered container and refrigerated for up to 1 week.) Serve at room temperature.

Shrimp and Corn Cakes with BBQ Rémoulade (or Pico de Gallo)

BBQ Rémoulade

½ cup mayonnaise

½ cup barbecue sauce (whatever kind you like best)

2 tablespoons dill pickle relish

1 tablespoon chopped drained capers

2 tablespoons chopped fresh chives

1 tablespoon grainy Dijon mustard

Corn Cakes

¾ cup all-purpose flour

¾ cup yellow cornmeal

1 teaspoon kosher salt

1 teaspoon freshly ground black pepper

½ teaspoon smoked paprika

1 cup canned cream-style corn

1 cup corn kernels, fresh or thawed frozen

3 large eggs

¾ cup whole milk

3 tablespoons unsalted butter, melted and cooled slightly

1 pound medium shrimp, peeled and deveined

1 cup shredded mozzarella cheese

1 cup shredded cheddar cheese

¼ cup finely chopped scallions, white and green parts, plus more for garnish

¼ cup finely chopped fresh parsley

Vegetable oil, for the griddle

Pico de Gallo (recipe follows), for serving (optional)

SERVES 6 TO 8 My love for corn cakes runs deep. With crispy outer edges and sweet, corn-filled centers, serve them for a brunch or supper or cook them as mini cakes to pass as party appetizers. Maybe the best way is to assemble a large platter of these pretties with a bowl of the BBQ rémoulade or Pico de Gallo (page 61) in the center and let everyone have at it.

---

1. **MAKE THE BBQ RÉMOULADE:** In a small bowl, mix together the mayonnaise, barbecue sauce, relish, capers, chives, and mustard. Set aside.

2. **MAKE THE CORN CAKES:** Preheat the oven to 200°F. In a large bowl, whisk together the flour, cornmeal, salt, pepper, and smoked paprika.

3. In a food processor, combine the cream-style corn, corn kernels, eggs, milk, and melted butter and pulse until coarsely pureed. Add to the flour mixture and stir to combine.

4. In the food processor (no need to clean the bowl), pulse the shrimp until very finely chopped. Add the shrimp to the batter, along with the mozzarella, cheddar, scallions, and parsley and fold together just until combined.

5. Place a wire rack inside of a half-sheet pan and set near the stove. Heat a large griddle or nonstick skillet over medium heat. Using a wad of paper towels, grease the griddle with the oil. Using about ¼ cup for each, drop the batter onto the griddle. Cook until the edges turn golden brown and the tops are covered with bubbles, 2 to 3 minutes, adjusting the heat as needed. Flip the cakes over and cook until the other side is browned, 2 to 3 minutes more. Transfer to the rack on the half-sheet pan. Keep the cakes warm in the preheated oven while cooking the remaining cakes.

6. Transfer to a platter, garnish with some scallions, and serve warm with the rémoulade or pico de gallo, if using. (The corn cakes can be cooled, layered in an airtight container, and frozen for up to 3 months. To serve, reheat in a griddle or skillet.)

Continues

PICO DE GALLO

Makes about 4 cups

1 cup finely chopped red onion

¼ cup fresh lime juice

1 jalapeño pepper, seeded and finely chopped

1 garlic clove, finely chopped

½ teaspoon ground cumin

1½ pounds red tomatoes, seeded and cut into small dice

½ cup finely chopped fresh cilantro

Kosher salt

This is the fresh and chunky salsa that is a staple of Mexican cooking. Don't reserve it for food from south of the border. I like it as a topping for calzones, especially the Breakfast Calzones (page 44).

1. In a medium bowl, mix together the red onion, lime juice, jalapeño, garlic, and cumin and let stand for 10 minutes.

2. Add the tomatoes and cilantro and mix well. Season with salt. The salsa is best served the same day, or cover and refrigerate for up to 2 days.

Eggplant and Feta Fritters with Tzatziki

2 large eggplants (about 1½ pounds each)

Extra-virgin olive oil, for brushing

Kosher salt and freshly ground black pepper

2 cups panko bread crumbs

1 cup crumbled feta cheese

3 large eggs, lightly beaten

⅓ cup freshly grated Parmigiano-Reggiano cheese

2 scallions, white and green parts, thinly sliced

2 tablespoons chopped fresh mint

2 tablespoons finely chopped fresh parsley

1 tablespoon dried oregano

2 garlic cloves, minced

Finely grated zest of 1 lemon

¼ teaspoon crushed red pepper flakes

Vegetable oil, for shallow-frying

Tzatziki (recipe follows), for serving

1 lemon, cut into wedges, for serving

SERVES 6 TO 8 The combination of the roasted eggplant, salty feta, lemon zest, and all of the fresh herbs offers you an irresistible taste of the Mediterranean. They can be served as an appetizer, stuffed in a sandwich, or on top of a salad, but I dare you to not eat the entire batch right out of the skillet!

1. Preheat the oven to 350°F. Line a half-sheet pan with parchment paper.

2. Halve the eggplants lengthwise. Score the cut sides in a deep crosshatch pattern, spacing the cuts about 1 inch apart, being sure not to cut through the skin. Generously brush the scored side with oil and season with salt and pepper. Place the eggplant, scored-side down, on the prepared pan.

3. Bake until the eggplant collapses and is very tender, about 30 minutes. Remove the eggplants and reduce the oven temperature to 200°F.

4. Let the eggplant stand until cool enough to handle, about 10 minutes. Using a large spoon, scoop the flesh from the eggplant into a large bowl, discarding the skin. Using a large fork, coarsely mash the eggplant flesh. Add the panko, feta, eggs, Parmigiano, scallions, mint, parsley, oregano, garlic, lemon zest, 1 teaspoon salt, ¼ teaspoon pepper, and the pepper flakes. Let stand to firm up slightly, about 10 minutes.

5. Line another half-sheet pan with paper towels and place near the stove. Pour ¼ inch of oil into a large skillet. Heat over medium-high heat until the oil is shimmering.

6. Using two soup spoons, scoop up about 3 tablespoons of the eggplant mixture with one spoon, and use the other spoon to scrape and slide the batter into the hot oil. (The fritter should be about the size of a golf ball.) Slightly flatten the fritter with the back of the spoon. Repeat with enough fritters to fill the skillet without crowding. Fry until the undersides are golden brown, 2 to 3 minutes. Flip the fritters and continue frying until the other sides are golden brown, 2 to 3 minutes more. Using a slotted spoon, transfer the fritters to the paper towels to drain. Keep warm in the oven while frying the remaining fritters.

7. Sprinkle with salt and serve with tzatziki and lemon wedges.

TZATZIKI

Makes about 3 cups

1 large standard cucumber

2 cups plain Greek low-fat yogurt

3 tablespoons extra-virgin olive oil

2 tablespoons finely chopped fresh dill

2 tablespoon red wine vinegar

1 tablespoon finely chopped fresh mint

1 tablespoon fresh lemon juice

2 garlic cloves, finely grated on a Microplane

Pinch of crushed red pepper flakes

Kosher salt and freshly ground black pepper

One of the best-known of Greece's culinary exports, creamy and herbaceous tzatziki needs one trick to make it successful: Always squeeze out the excess water from the cucumber, or the dip will thin out as it stands. This is another big-batch dip that I always make in quantity because it is so useful with raw veggies and even as a chunky sauce for grilled salmon or lamb chops.

1. Peel the cucumber. Grate the cucumber flesh on the large holes of a box grater, down to, and discarding, the seedy center. A handful at a time, squeeze out the excess water, transferring the cucumber flesh to a medium bowl.

2. Add the yogurt, oil, dill, vinegar, mint, lemon juice, garlic, and pepper flakes and stir well. Season with salt and black pepper. Cover and refrigerate for 30 minutes to 1 hour to chill and blend the flavors.

3. The tzatziki can be refrigerated for up to 3 days. Stir before serving.

Buttermilk Galette Dough

1¼ cups all-purpose flour, plus more for rolling

1½ teaspoons sugar

½ teaspoon kosher salt

1 stick (4 ounces) cold unsalted butter, cubed

5 tablespoons buttermilk (see Note), as needed

Note

Buttermilk is acidic and helps to tenderize the gluten in the flour. Get in the habit of keeping buttermilk in the fridge. It is fermented, and therefore keeps longer than the use-by date on the carton, at least in my experience. Admittedly, though, I tend to use it up in Ranch Dressing (page 131), the Ham, Cheese, and Chive Muffins (page 43), and for precoating chicken before dipping in flour or crumbs for cooking (Cornflake Chicken Tenders with Campfire BBQ Sauce on page 91). Buttermilk also shows up in cake and other baked goods not in this book. It doesn't have time to go bad! If you don't have buttermilk, mix 1 tablespoon distilled white or cider vinegar or lemon juice into 1 cup of 2% or whole milk and let stand until curdled, about 5 minutes.

MAKES ENOUGH FOR ONE 9-INCH GALETTE There are so many things to love about this recipe, I don't know where to start. First of all, buttermilk is the secret ingredient that gives the dough a great crumb and makes it versatile—at once tangy and sweet. Then, the butter makes the dough flaky and brings crisp edges and flavor. You can also add various herbs to the dough—see the Herbed Galette Dough variation that follows.

1. **TO MAKE IN A FOOD PROCESSOR:** In a food processor, pulse the flour, sugar, and salt. Add the butter and pulse about 5 times until the mixture looks like coarse meal with some pea-sized bits of butter. Remove the lid and drizzle 4 tablespoons of the buttermilk all over the flour mixture. Then cover and pulse just until the dough comes together, adding more buttermilk if needed.

2. **TO MAKE THE DOUGH BY HAND:** In a bowl, mix together the flour, sugar, and salt. Using a large serving fork or pastry blender, cut in the butter until the mixture resembles coarse meal with some pea-sized bits of butter. Gradually stir in the buttermilk, adding just enough for the dough to hold together when pressed in your fist.

3. Turn out the dough onto a lightly floured work surface. Press and shape the dough into a flat disk, wrap in plastic, and refrigerate until chilled, about 1 hour. (The dough can be made up to 2 days ahead. Let stand at room temperature for 15 minutes before rolling out.)

VARIATION

Herbed Galette Dough: You can add herbs according to whim and what you have on hand, but I find rosemary and thyme to be the most useful for savory galettes. Add 2 teaspoons finely chopped fresh rosemary, thyme, basil, or mint to the flour before processing with (or cutting in) the butter. This allows the herb flavor to infuse the other ingredients.

Savory Fig, Goat Cheese, and Onion Galette

Herbed Galette Dough (page 64, made with rosemary) or 1 round store-bought refrigerated pie dough

All-purpose flour, for rolling

½ cup crumbled goat cheese

3 tablespoons balsamic vinegar

½ cup Caramelized Onions (page 84)

20 fresh figs (about 2 pounds), cut into quarters

Egg wash: 1 large egg beaten with 1 teaspoon water or milk

Honey, for drizzling

SERVES 8 Legit, my heart skips a little bit whenever figs are involved. And I totally get this from my dad. I developed this tart recipe for my father because he loved figs more than anyone I know. And what Dad wanted, Dad got!

1. Preheat the oven to 350°F. Line a half-sheet pan with parchment paper.

2. Place the dough on a lightly floured work surface. Sprinkle flour on top. Roll out the dough into a 12-inch round (it doesn't have to be perfectly round). Transfer to the prepared half-sheet pan. Sprinkle half of the goat cheese over the round, leaving a 2½-inch border around the circumference.

3. In a small bowl, stir the balsamic vinegar into the onions. Scatter them over the cheese. Heap the figs over the cheese. Fold the crust up and over the filling where it meets the filling, pleating the dough as needed. Sprinkle the remaining goat cheese over the filling. Brush the crust with the egg wash.

4. Bake until the crust is golden, about 40 minutes.

5. Drizzle with honey and serve hot, warm, or cooled.

Clockwise, from left: Potato, Onion, and Gruyère Galette (page 69); Savory Fig, Goat Cheese, and Onion Galette (page 65); and Springtime Galette with Green Goddess Dressing (page 68)

Springtime Galette with Green Goddess Dressing

2 tablespoons unsalted butter

1 tablespoon olive oil

1 cup chopped leeks, white and pale-green parts only, rinsed well

1 garlic clove, finely chopped

1 teaspoon finely chopped fresh thyme

Kosher salt and freshly ground black pepper

¼ teaspoon crushed red pepper flakes

1 8-ounce package thawed frozen artichoke hearts

6 ounces asparagus spears, trimmed, cut into 2-inch pieces

½ cup green peas, fresh or thawed frozen

2 tablespoons finely chopped fresh dill

All-purpose flour, for rolling the dough

Buttermilk Galette Dough (page 64) or 1 round store-bought refrigerated pie dough

1 cup shredded fontina cheese

1 tablespoon heavy cream

Green Goddess Dressing (page 230), for serving

SERVES 6 TO 8 This vegetable-forward galette is the perfect recipe when you're craving a totally impressive meal that screams spring. Easy to throw together, it's loaded with tender fresh green produce and flavorful cheese all wrapped in a golden buttery crust. This is even simpler to do if you have a frozen galette crust already made in your freezer! Pair it with a simple green salad as a main, or slice it up and serve as a side to any protein.

1. Melt the butter and oil in a large skillet over medium heat. Add the leeks, garlic, and thyme and cook, stirring occasionally, until the leeks soften, 4 to 5 minutes.

2. Season with salt and pepper and add the red pepper flakes. Add the artichoke hearts, asparagus, peas, and dill. Cover and cook, stirring often, until the leeks are tender, about 3 minutes. Transfer the vegetables to a plate and let stand, stirring occasionally, until cool. It's best to let the vegetables cool completely, but if you're short on time, then allow them to cool for at least 15 minutes.

3. Preheat the oven to 425°F. Line a half-sheet pan with parchment paper.

4. Place the dough on a lightly floured work surface. Sprinkle flour on top. Roll out the dough into a 12-inch round (it doesn't have to be perfect). Transfer to the prepared half-sheet pan. Sprinkle half of the fontina over the round, leaving a 2½-inch border around the circumference. Spread the vegetables over the cheese. Sprinkle with the remaining fontina. Fold the crust up and over the filling where it meets the filling, pleating the dough as needed. Brush the crust with the heavy cream.

5. Bake until the crust is golden, about 40 minutes.

6. Cut the galette into wedges and serve with the dressing drizzled on top.

Potato, Onion, and Gruyère Galette

3 large Yukon Gold potatoes (15 ounces total), scrubbed but unpeeled

2 tablespoons olive oil

½ teaspoon kosher salt

⅛ teaspoon freshly ground black pepper

Herbed Galette Dough (page 64, made with thyme) or 1 round store-bought refrigerated pie dough

Flour, for rolling

1 cup shredded Gruyère cheese

½ cup Caramelized Onions (page 84)

Egg wash: 1 large egg beaten with 1 teaspoon water

Fresh thyme sprigs, for garnish, optional

SERVES 6 TO 8 This galette is inspired by savory Mediterranean flavors, and a carb lover's dream (count me in). While the tart is vegetable-based, I often serve a platter of crisp bacon and/or plump browned sausages alongside for the meat-eaters at the table. For easy assembly in the morning, make and chill the dough, caramelize the onions, and parcook the potatoes the night before. With these steps done, you can have this ready for the oven before you've had your morning coffee.

1. Using a mandoline, plastic V-slicer, or a large knife, cut the potatoes into thin rounds.

2. Heat the oil in a large skillet over medium-high heat. Add the potatoes and sprinkle with the salt and pepper. Cover and cook, stirring occasionally, until the potatoes are softened and just beginning to brown, about 10 minutes. Transfer to a plate and let cool. (The parcooked potatoes can be covered and refrigerated up to 1 day.)

3. Preheat the oven to 350°F. Line a half-sheet pan with parchment paper.

4. Place the dough on a lightly floured work surface. Sprinkle flour on top. Roll out the dough into a 12-inch round (it doesn't have to be perfect). Transfer to the prepared half-sheet pan. Sprinkle half of the Gruyère over the dough, leaving a 2½-inch border around the circumference. Top with overlapping potato rounds in concentric circles. Scatter the caramelized onions on top. Sprinkle with the remaining cheese. Fold the crust up and over the filling where it meets the filling, pleating the dough as needed. Brush the crust with the egg wash. Sprinkle the remaining cheese all over the galette, including the crust.

5. Bake until the crust is golden, about 40 minutes.

6. Serve hot, warm, or cooled, garnished with thyme sprigs, if you'd like.

Chicken Fajita Pinwheels

1 tablespoon vegetable oil

2 red or green bell peppers, preferably 1 each, cut into thin strips

1 large yellow onion, cut into thin half-moons

3 garlic cloves, thinly sliced

1 jalapeño pepper, seeded and finely chopped

3 cups shredded cooked chicken (rotisserie chicken is fine)

3/4 cup Enchilada Sauce, homemade (page 162) or store-bought

Kosher salt

Cooking spray

Flour, for rolling out the dough

1 pound refrigerated pizza dough (see page 45), at room temperature

3 cups shredded Mexican-blend or mozzarella cheese

2 tablespoons chili powder

2 teaspoons ground cumin

Chopped fresh cilantro, for sprinkling (optional)

MAKES 9 PINWHEELS (SERVES 4 TO 6) These pastry pinwheels are a mash-up of two of my family's favorite things, pizza and chicken fajitas. Pizza dough is filled like savory cinnamon rolls, sliced, and baked until golden and melty. They can be served on their own or with a side bowl of Enchilada Sauce (page 162) or Avocado Lime Crema (page 162) for dunking.

1. Heat the oil in a large skillet over medium heat. Add the bell peppers, onion, garlic, and jalapeño and cook, stirring occasionally, until softened, about 5 minutes. Remove from the heat and stir in the chicken and enchilada sauce. Season with salt. Let cool until tepid, about 20 minutes.

2. Preheat the oven to 400°F. Mist a half-sheet pan with the cooking spray.

3. On a lightly floured work surface, roll out the dough into a 10 × 15-inch rectangle, with the long side facing you. Sprinkle half of the shredded cheese over the dough, leaving a 1-inch border. Top with the chicken mixture. Sprinkle the remaining cheese over the chicken, then sprinkle with the chili powder and cumin. Starting on a long side, tightly roll up the dough into a tight cylinder and pinch the seam closed. Using a sharp knife, cut the roll crosswise into 9 equal rounds. Arrange the rounds, cut-side up, on the prepared pan.

4. Bake until golden brown, 20 to 25 minutes. Sprinkle with the cilantro, if using, and serve.

VARIATION

BBQ Chicken Roll-Ups: Substitute barbecue sauce for the enchilada sauce, and shredded Monterey Jack for the Mexican cheese blend. Omit the chili powder and cumin.

Butter Chicken Calzones

Butter Chicken

2 tablespoons unsalted butter

2 tablespoons olive oil, plus more as needed

1½ pounds boneless, skinless chicken breast, cut into 1-inch chunks

Kosher salt and freshly ground black pepper

1 yellow onion, chopped

1 tablespoon finely chopped peeled fresh ginger

4 garlic cloves, minced

6 tablespoons tomato paste

1 4-ounce jar Thai red curry paste (about ½ cup)

1 tablespoon garam masala

1 tablespoon Madras-style curry powder

1 teaspoon chili powder

1 teaspoon yellow mustard seeds, coarsely ground (see Note)

1 teaspoon coriander seeds, coarsely ground (see Note)

¼ teaspoon cayenne pepper

1 14-ounce can coconut milk

1 cup thawed frozen peas

¼ cup finely chopped fresh cilantro

Calzones

1 pound refrigerated pizza dough (see page 45), at room temperature

Flour, for rolling the dough

2 cups shredded mozzarella cheese

Olive oil, for brushing

MAKES 2 LARGE CALZONES (SERVES 6 TO 8) Butter chicken is an iconic Indian dish of boneless chicken in a spicy, creamy, luscious sauce. It's typically eaten with rice or naan to sop up all of the delicious gravy. But, by using pizza dough to encase the chicken, we're eliminating the need for any other bread. Slice open the calzone and a rush of aromatic butter chicken erupts, spilling out onto the plate, ready to get mopped up by the pizza crust. It's a perfect food mash-up.

1. **MAKE THE BUTTER CHICKEN:** Heat the butter and oil together in a large saucepan or Dutch oven over medium-high heat. Season the chicken with 2 teaspoons salt and ½ teaspoon pepper. In batches, add the chicken to the pan and cook, stirring occasionally, until seared on all sides, adding more oil as needed, about 6 minutes. Using a slotted spoon, transfer the seared chicken to a bowl.

2. Add the onion, ginger, and garlic to the saucepan and cook, stirring occasionally, until the onion softens, about 3 minutes. Stir in the tomato paste, red curry paste, garam masala, curry powder, chili powder, mustard seeds, coriander seeds, and cayenne and cook, stirring often, until the mixture deepens in color, about 2 minutes.

3. Add the coconut milk to the pan and stir with a wooden spoon to scrape up the spice mixture on the bottom. Return the chicken and its juices to the saucepan and stir well. Bring the sauce to a boil. And then immediately reduce the heat to medium-low and simmer, uncovered, stirring occasionally, until the chicken is just cooked through and the sauce is thickened, about 20 minutes.

4. Remove from the heat and cool completely. Stir in the peas and cilantro. (To speed cooling, spread the filling out in a half-sheet pan or large baking dish and stir often. The butter chicken can be cooled, covered, and refrigerated for up to 1 day.)

5. **ASSEMBLE THE CALZONES:** Position the rack in the top third of the oven and preheat the oven to 425°F. Line a half-sheet pan with parchment paper.

6. Cut the pizza dough in half and shape each into a ball. For each calzone, on a lightly floured work surface, roll out a ball of dough into a 12-inch round. Transfer the round to one of the sheet pans. Spoon

half of the filling on the bottom half of the round, leaving a ½-inch border, and sprinkle with ½ cup of the mozzarella. Fold the dough in half to enclose the filling. Pinch and pleat the edges together to seal. Repeat with the remaining dough, filling, and cheese, building the second calzone on the second prepared pan. Lightly brush the calzones with olive oil and cut a couple of slits on top of each as vents.

7. Bake the calzones until they are golden brown, 20 to 25 minutes.

8. Let cool slightly. Cut crosswise directly on the half-sheet pan into individual servings and serve hot.

Note

Grind the whole spices in a clean blade-style coffee grinder, in a mortar with a pestle, or crush them as finely as possible on a work surface underneath a heavy saucepan. You aren't going for finely ground in this recipe, so any of these methods will work well. (For finely ground, stick to the coffee grinder.)

Pizza Pockets

Pizza Sauce

1 28-ounce can crushed tomatoes

2 tablespoons tomato paste

2 tablespoons olive oil

½ teaspoon dried oregano

Kosher salt

Pockets

All-purpose flour, for rolling the dough

1 pound refrigerated pizza dough (see page 45), at room temperature

½ cup finely chopped pepperoni

½ cup diced green bell pepper

½ cup sliced black olives

½ cup chopped red onion

1 cup shredded low-moisture mozzarella cheese

⅓ cup freshly grated Parmigiano-Reggiano cheese

1 teaspoon dried oregano

Egg wash: 1 large egg beaten with 1 teaspoon water

1 tablespoon sesame seeds

MAKES 6 POCKETS Pizza pockets are fun to make, and little kids love to get involved to help. You can make them vegetarian by swapping cooked mushrooms for the pepperoni or if everyone is meat-leaning, then use a mixture of your favorite Italian-style meat or sausage instead of going with just the pepperoni.

1. **MAKE THE PIZZA SAUCE:** In a small saucepan, whisk together the crushed tomatoes, tomato paste, oil, and oregano. Bring to a simmer over medium heat. Reduce the heat to low, cover, and simmer, stirring often, until slightly reduced, about 10 minutes. Season with salt. Transfer about ¾ cup of the sauce to a small bowl and let it cool. Cover the remaining sauce to keep warm to serve as a dip.

2. **MAKE THE POCKETS:** Preheat the oven to 450°F. Line a half-sheet pan with parchment paper.

3. On a lightly floured work surface, roll out the dough into a 10 × 15-inch rectangle. With a long side facing you, use a large knife or a pizza wheel, cut the dough crosswise into thirds, and then in half lengthwise to make six 5-inch squares. Spoon about 2 tablespoons of the cooled sauce over each dough square, spreading it with the back of a spoon and leaving a 1-inch border around the edges.

4. In a small bowl, combine the pepperoni, bell pepper, olives, and onion. Divide the mixture evenly among the squares. In another small bowl, mix the mozzarella, Parmigiano, and oregano. Divide over the vegetables.

5. For each pocket, bring the four corners of the dough up to meet in the center of the square and pinch the seams closed to cover the filling. Transfer to the half-sheet pan. Brush with the egg wash and sprinkle with sesame seeds.

6. Bake until golden brown, 15 to 20 minutes.

7. If desired, reheat the remaining sauce in the saucepan. Serve the pockets with the warm sauce.

Muhammara with Cumin Pita Chips

Muhammara

2 slices crusty bread, preferably day-old, torn into chunks

1 12-ounce jar roasted red peppers, drained

1/2 cup walnuts, toasted lightly (see Notes), plus more for garnish

3 garlic cloves, smashed and peeled

2 tablespoons fresh lemon juice

1 1/2 tablespoons pomegranate molasses (see Notes)

1 teaspoon Aleppo pepper (see Notes), plus more for garnish

1 teaspoon ground cumin

1/2 teaspoon smoked paprika

1/4 teaspoon crushed red pepper flakes

1/2 cup extra-virgin olive oil

Kosher salt and freshly ground black pepper

Cumin Pita Chips

3 pitas, each cut into 8 wedges, layers separated to make 48 pieces

1/4 cup olive oil

1 teaspoon ground cumin

1 teaspoon kosher salt

1/2 teaspoon freshly ground black pepper

Pomegranate arils (seeds) (optional)

Chopped walnuts (optional)

Aleppo pepper (optional)

MAKES ABOUT 2 CUPS DIP (6 TO 8 SERVINGS) Muhammara, made with red pepper and walnuts, is a Syrian spread/dip/what-have-you, and is the reason why I always have a bottle of pomegranate molasses in my fridge. The dip covers all the flavor bases—it's sweet, slightly smoky, and a little bit spicy. I love to serve it with these cumin pita chips or as part of a crudités platter. It's also terrific spread on a sandwich or burger, folded into an omelet, served over a frittata, or spooned over grilled fish or chicken. If you can, make it a day ahead for the flavors to meld before serving.

1. **MAKE THE MUHAMMARA:** Process the crusty bread in a food processor to make coarse bread crumbs. Measure out 2/3 cup and save the remaining bread crumbs for another use (like meatballs or meatloaf).

2. Return the 2/3 cup bread crumbs to the food processor and add the roasted peppers, walnuts, garlic, lemon juice, pomegranate molasses, Aleppo pepper, cumin, smoked paprika, and red pepper flakes and pulse until coarsely chopped. With the machine running, gradually add the oil and process until smooth. Season with salt and black pepper. Transfer to a covered container and refrigerate for at least 2 hours or up to 5 days.

3. **MAKE THE CUMIN PITA CHIPS:** Preheat the oven to 400°F.

4. Arrange the pita wedges on a half-sheet pan. Drizzle with the oil. In a small bowl, mix the cumin, salt, and pepper. Sprinkle over the pita and toss well. Spread the pita out in a single layer.

5. Bake for 6 minutes. Flip the pitas and continue baking until golden brown, 5 to 6 minutes more.

6. Let cool. (The pita chips can be stored in paper bags for up to 2 days at room temperature.)

7. For a gorgeous presentation, transfer the muhammara to a serving bowl and sprinkle with pomegranate arils, chopped walnuts, and Aleppo pepper, if desired, and serve with the cumin chips.

Notes

- To toast nuts, heat a small skillet over medium heat. Add the nuts and cook, stirring occasionally, until fragrant and lightly toasted, 2 to 3 minutes. Nuts can burn easily, and they don't all cook at the same time, so watch closely. Some nuts will take more or less time.

- Pomegranate molasses is sold at Middle Eastern groceries or online.

- Aleppo pepper is a mildly hot, fruity red chile that is dried and flaked. Commonplace crushed red pepper flakes are spicier but can be substituted to taste.

White Bean and Roasted Garlic Dip

2 15-ounce cans cannellini (white kidney beans), drained and rinsed

½ cup extra-virgin olive oil

⅓ cup packed fresh parsley

1 tablespoon mashed Roasted Garlic (recipe follows) or 3 smashed and peeled raw garlic cloves

Finely grated zest and juice of 1 lemon

2 tablespoons hot water

1 teaspoon coarsely chopped fresh thyme

Pinch of crushed red pepper flakes

Kosher salt and freshly ground black pepper

MAKES ABOUT 3 CUPS Here is a hearty and healthy staple to love. If I am entertaining and I can only make one dip, more than likely this is it. Make a double batch so you have extra on hand for lots of uses.

In a food processor, combine the beans, oil, parsley, garlic, lemon zest, lemon juice, hot water, thyme, and pepper flakes. Pulse until coarsely chopped. Season with salt and pepper. Adjust the thickness with additional oil, lemon juice, or water, if needed. (The dip can be stored in a covered container for up to 1 week.)

ROASTED GARLIC

Makes about ⅓ cup mashed garlic

4 large, plump heads garlic

Olive oil, for drizzling and storage

Kosher salt and freshly ground black pepper

Whenever I roast garlic, I always make several heads at a time—it's so good and I use it in many different ways—in mashed potatoes, mac and cheese, sauces, gravies, sandwiches, dressings, and dips. Here's a use I bet you didn't know: Mix mashed roasted garlic with mayo and spread on the Thanksgiving turkey before roasting for a beautiful brown glaze.

1. Preheat the oven to 350°F. Using a large knife, cut the top ½ inch from each head of garlic. Place a head, cut-side up, on a square of foil. Drizzle oil over the cut top and season with a pinch each of salt and pepper. Wrap the garlic in the foil. Repeat with the remaining garlic. Place the wrapped garlic on a half-sheet pan.

2. Bake until the garlic cloves are very tender and a gorgeous golden brown (open the foil to check), about 45 minutes.

3. Unwrap the garlic and let cool until easy to handle. Squeeze the flesh from the garlic hulls into a bowl, discarding the hulls. Transfer to a covered container, pour a thin layer of oil over the top, and refrigerate. (The mashed garlic can be refrigerated for up to 2 weeks.)

Marinated Goat Cheese with Crostini

Marinated Goat Cheese

1 4-ounce log goat cheese

1/2 cup extra-virgin olive oil, as needed

1 scallion, white and green parts, thinly sliced

3 tablespoons coarsely chopped marinated sun-dried tomatoes

2 tablespoons finely chopped fresh dill

Kosher salt and freshly ground black pepper

Crushed red pepper flakes

Crostini

1 baguette

1/4 cup extra-virgin olive oil

Kosher salt and freshly ground black pepper

SERVES 6 TO 8 I could eat this every day. In fact, there was a time that I actually did. When I worked at Whole Foods, we made this incredible marinated goat cheese that I was obsessed with and I still am. This recipe, fragrant with dill, is the one that I used back then, but you can switch out different herbs like basil, thyme, or oregano, or use a combination. Allow the cheese to marinate at least 1 hour (overnight is better) before serving. A 1-pint canning jar or deli container works well for marinating and storing the cheese.

1. **MARINATE THE GOAT CHEESE:** Cut the goat cheese in half—dental floss does a great job. Pour about 1 tablespoon of oil into a 1-pint canning jar or deli container. Add the cheese, one on top of the other. Add the scallion, sun-dried tomatoes, and dill. Add a pinch of salt, a grind or two of black pepper, and a pinch of red pepper flakes to the jar. Pour in enough oil to cover the cheese. Cover and let stand at room temperature for least 1 hour. (The cheese can be refrigerated for up to 2 weeks.)

2. **BAKE THE CROSTINI:** Preheat the oven to 375°F. Using a serrated knife held on a slight diagonal, cut the baguette into 1/2-inch slices. Arrange the slices in a single layer on a half-sheet pan. Brush with the oil. Season with salt and pepper.

3. Bake for 6 minutes. Flip the crostini and continue baking until crisp and golden, about 6 minutes more. Let cool.

4. If the marinated cheese has been refrigerated, about 1 hour before serving, let it stand at room temperature to liquefy the chilled oil.

5. Transfer to a shallow serving bowl with some of the oil and seasonings. Serve the cheese with the crostini.

Sleeping Dogs with Caramelized Onions

All-purpose flour, for rolling out the pastry

1 17.3-ounce box frozen puff pastry (2 sheets), such as Pepperidge Farm, thawed (see Note, page 85)

8 tablespoons stone-ground mustard

2 cups Caramelized Onions (recipe follows)

8 hot dogs

Egg wash: 1 large egg beaten with 1 teaspoon water

Poppy or sesame seeds (optional), for sprinkling

2 tablespoons finely chopped fresh chives

Honey Dijon Dipping Sauce

½ cup mayonnaise

¼ cup honey

¼ cup smooth or stone-ground mustard

2 tablespoons fresh lemon juice

MAKES 8 There was one given at dinner time with my small kids: Put out a tray of pigs in a blanket, and they would be snarfed down in minutes. These days not much has changed, except that I'm taking a few more liberties. Here I've developed a fun and delicious riff on the classic snack: Full hot dogs are nestled in a bed of caramelized onions (see recipe on page 84) and wrapped up in a blanket of flaky, buttery puff pastry before being baked until golden and then dipped in a spicy honey mustard sauce. Still "pigs in a blanket," but all grown up.

1. Preheat the oven to 425°F. Line a half-sheet pan with parchment paper.

2. On a lightly floured surface, gently roll each pastry sheet into a 10-inch square to remove the creases. Cut each sheet into four 5-inch squares, making a total of eight 5-inch squares.

3. Spread 1 tablespoon of mustard on each square, leaving a ½-inch border. Spread ¼ cup of the onions vertically down the center of the mustard in a column and top with a hot dog. Fold one side of the pastry over to cover the hot dog, then continue rolling. Brush the end with the egg wash as you finish the roll to glue the seam closed. Place, seam-side down, on the prepared pan. Repeat with the remaining ingredients.

4. Cut a couple of slits in the top of each pastry, brush with the egg wash, and sprinkle with sesame seeds. Bake until puffed and golden brown, 20 to 25 minutes. Sprinkle with chives.

5. **MEANWHILE, MAKE THE DIPPING SAUCE:** In a small bowl, whisk together the mayonnaise, honey, mustard, and lemon juice.

6. Serve the pastries hot, with the dipping sauce on the side.

Continues

CARAMELIZED ONIONS

Makes about 2 cups

2 tablespoons unsalted butter

2½ pounds Spanish (yellow) onions (about 3 large), cut into ⅛- to ¼-inch half-moons

Kosher salt and freshly ground black pepper

Caramelized onions are literally gold in your kitchen. There are so many things to do with them, beyond using them as a topping for burgers and sandwiches. I have lots of recipes where I add onions for their deep, complex mix of sweet and savory flavors. I highly recommend making a batch—whenever you know you're going to be near the stove (so you can keep an eye on them)—to have in the fridge to use as needed.

1. Melt the butter in a large saucepan (preferably nonstick) over medium heat. Add the onions, season with ½ teaspoon salt and ¼ teaspoon pepper, cover, and cook, stirring occasionally, until the onions have wilted down and begin to brown, about 10 minutes.

2. Uncover, reduce the heat to medium-low, and cook, stirring every 10 to 15 minutes, until the onions are very tender, greatly reduced in volume, and are deep beige, 40 to 50 minutes. Do not rush this process, and adjust the heat as needed so the onions don't burn.

3. Season with additional salt and pepper. Let the onions cool, then store in an airtight container in the refrigerator for up to 1 week.

Antipasto Torta

All-purpose flour, for rolling out the pastry

1 17.3-ounce package (2 sheets) frozen puff pastry, such as Pepperidge Farm, thawed (see Note)

2 tablespoons Dijon mustard

8 thin slices mortadella, bologna, or boiled ham

12 thin slices salami

12 thin slices soppressata

8 thin slices provolone

4 ounces mozzarella cheese, thinly sliced

2 cups baby spinach

1/3 cup chopped jarred roasted red pepper, patted dry

1/4 cup sliced pitted black olives

1 teaspoon dried oregano

Egg wash: 1 large egg beaten with 1 teaspoon water

Sesame seeds, for sprinkling

SERVES 6 TO 8 This antipasto torta can be filled with your favorite cured meats, cheeses, and vegetables and baked into crispy flaky goodness. It's also a great way to use up any bits and pieces from the deli, and you can use any combination of Italian meats you like. Cut a big square and serve alongside a salad for dinner, or slice into smaller squares as an appetizer to enjoy with a glass of wine.

1. Preheat the oven to 425°F. Line a half-sheet pan with parchment paper.

2. On a lightly floured work surface, roll out one of the pastry sheets to a 10 × 12-inch rectangle. Transfer to the prepared pan. Brush the mustard in the center of the pastry, leaving a 1-inch border. Shingle the mortadella, salami, soppressata, and provolone over the mustard. Top with the mozzarella and the spinach. Sprinkle the roasted pepper on top and sprinkle with the olives and oregano. Brush the exposed border with the egg wash.

3. Roll out the second pastry sheet into an 11 × 13-inch rectangle (to fit over the heaping toppings). Center over the first rectangle and press and seal the edges together with a fork. Cut a few slits in the top to allow the steam to escape. Brush with the egg wash and sprinkle with sesame seeds.

4. Bake until golden brown, about 25 minutes.

Note

When I began catering, I discovered the joys of frozen puff pastry, and I've never looked back. It's incredibly easy to use. Your supermarket no doubt carries frozen Pepperidge Farm puff pastry, which I love because it is easy to find and very reliable. Follow the package directions to thaw the dough. You will see marks where the dough was folded, but these roll out easily. Remember, puff pastry should always be kept cold.

Antipasto Torta (page 85)

Sweet and Savory Pear and Gorgonzola Tart

All-purpose flour, for rolling the dough

Half a 17.3-ounce package (1 sheet) frozen puff pastry, such as Pepperidge Farm, thawed (see Note, page 85)

2 Comice or Anjou pears, unpeeled

2 tablespoons fresh lemon juice

½ cup crumbled Gorgonzola or other blue cheese

¼ cup coarsely chopped toasted walnuts

2 tablespoons turbinado sugar

Egg wash: 1 large egg beaten with 1 teaspoon water

Honey, for drizzling

About ½ teaspoon cracked black peppercorns (coarsely crushed with a mortar and pestle or under a small saucepan)

About 2 teaspoons finely chopped fresh rosemary

SERVES 6 I am such a sucker for the flavor combination of pears and Gorgonzola cheese, and this magic duo stars as the topping for this quick tart. The salty creamy cheese pairs beautifully with the sweet juiciness of the pears with the added benefit of a drizzle of honey and a finish of crunchy walnuts. Yep, it's party-in-your-mouth perfection.

1. Preheat the oven to 450°F. Line a half-sheet pan with parchment paper.

2. On a lightly floured work surface, gently roll the pastry into an 11-inch square. Transfer to the prepared half-sheet pan. Using a small sharp knife, score a 1-inch border around the edges of the square, like a frame, taking care not to cut through the pastry. Using a fork, thoroughly pierce the inside of the center area inside the "frame."

3. Cut the pears in quarters lengthwise. Trim off the thick core from each quarter, then thinly slice the pears lengthwise. Place in a small bowl and gently toss with the lemon juice.

4. Sprinkle the center of the pastry, inside the frame, with the Gorgonzola and walnuts. Shingle the pears inside the frame. Sprinkle with the sugar. Brush the pastry border with the egg wash.

5. Bake until the pastry is puffed and golden brown, about 20 minutes.

6. Let cool for 5 minutes. Slide onto a serving platter. Drizzle with honey and sprinkle with the cracked pepper and rosemary. Serve hot, warm, or at room temperature.

Cornflake Chicken Tenders with Campfire BBQ Sauce

Campfire BBQ Sauce

½ cup mayonnaise

½ cup hickory barbecue sauce

2 teaspoons spicy brown mustard

2 teaspoons honey

½ teaspoon chipotle powder

½ teaspoon smoked paprika

½ teaspoon kosher salt

Chicken Tenders

2½ pounds boneless, skinless chicken breasts

1 cup buttermilk

2 teaspoons hot sauce, such as Tabasco

2 tablespoons dill pickle brine

½ teaspoon smoked paprika

Kosher salt and freshly ground black pepper

4½ cups cornflakes

½ teaspoon garlic powder

¼ teaspoon onion powder

Olive oil or avocado oil spray

Finely chopped fresh parsley, for serving

SERVES 8 TO 10 These tender and juicy baked chicken pieces are coated in a crunchy cornflake crust, which adds an unexpected sweetness and gives us that golden and crispy exterior that my family craves. And these tenders are so versatile. Serve them over a green salad with the BBQ sauce as a dressing, or make into an outrageous sandwich with some cheese, pickles, and the smoky sauce.

1. **MAKE THE CAMPFIRE BBQ SAUCE:** In a small bowl, whisk together the mayonnaise, barbecue sauce, mustard, honey, chipotle, smoked paprika, and salt. Cover and refrigerate until ready to serve. (The sauce can be covered and refrigerated for up to 3 days. Let it come to room temperature before serving.)

2. **MARINATE THE CHICKEN TENDERS:** Pound the chicken breasts to a ½-inch thickness (see Note, page 101), then cut into strips about ¾ inch wide.

3. In a large glass, ceramic, or stainless steel bowl, whisk together the buttermilk, hot sauce, pickle brine, smoked paprika, 1 teaspoon salt, and ½ teaspoon black pepper. Add the chicken strips and stir to coat. Cover with plastic wrap and refrigerate for 1 to 2 hours.

4. Put the cornflakes in a 1-gallon resealable plastic bag and finely crush them with a rolling pin. Add the garlic powder, onion powder, ½ teaspoon salt, and ½ teaspoon black pepper and shake to mix.

5. Preheat the oven to 400°F. Mist a large half-sheet pan with cooking spray.

6. A few at a time, remove the chicken from the marinade, shake off the excess liquid, and add to the bag of seasoned cornflakes. Shake to coat. Transfer to the half-sheet pan. Mist lightly with olive oil or avocado oil spray.

7. Bake for 10 minutes. Remove from the oven. Turn the chicken over and mist again with cooking spray. Return to the oven and bake until the crust is set, 5 to 10 minutes. Sprinkle with the parsley and serve hot, with the BBQ sauce for dipping.

Baked Coconut Shrimp with Pineapple Chili Sauce

Pineapple Chili Sauce

½ cup pineapple juice

2½ tablespoons light brown sugar

2 tablespoons soy sauce

2 tablespoons Thai sweet chili sauce

½ teaspoon grated fresh ginger, grated on a Microplane

½ garlic clove, grated on a Microplane

¾ teaspoon cornstarch

Shrimp

Cooking spray

½ cup all-purpose flour

½ teaspoon garlic powder

½ teaspoon smoked paprika

¼ teaspoon kosher salt

¼ teaspoon cayenne pepper

⅛ teaspoon freshly ground black pepper

2 large eggs

1 cup coconut flakes (sweetened or unsweetened)

½ cup panko bread crumbs

1 tablespoon sesame seeds

1 pound large (21/25 count) shrimp, peeled and deveined, tails left on

SERVES 4 TO 6 These crispy coconut shrimp are one of my favorite things to serve when we have guests because they can be prepared ahead of time and popped in the oven when ready to serve. The sauce can even be made the day before. They're golden and crunchy and guaranteed to be the first thing to go as soon as you pull them out of the oven!

1. **MAKE THE SAUCE:** In a small saucepan, combine the pineapple juice, brown sugar, soy sauce, Thai chili sauce, ginger, and garlic. Bring to a simmer over medium-high heat, stirring often.

2. Put 1 tablespoon water in a ramekin or small bowl, sprinkle in the cornstarch, and stir to dissolve. Stir into the pineapple mixture. Reduce the heat to low and simmer again until thickened, about 2 minutes. Transfer to a small bowl and let cool. (The sauce can be refrigerated in a covered container for up to 2 days. Let it come to room temperature before serving.)

3. **MAKE THE SHRIMP:** Preheat the oven to 425°F. Coat a half-sheet pan with cooking spray.

4. **SET UP A DREDGING STATION IN THREE SHALLOW BOWLS:** In one bowl, stir together the flour, garlic powder, smoked paprika, salt, cayenne, and black pepper. Beat the eggs in a second bowl. In the third bowl, mix the coconut, panko, and sesame seeds.

5. One at a time, coat the shrimp in the flour mixture, then the eggs, and then the panko. Transfer to the prepared half-sheet pan.

6. Mist the coated shrimp with the cooking spray. Bake until the shrimp are golden brown and opaque throughout, about 10 minutes. Serve hot, with the sauce for dipping.

Crispy Cod Sticks with Bang Bang Sauce

Bang Bang Sauce

1 cup mayonnaise

1/2 cup Thai sweet chili sauce

1 tablespoon sriracha

Kosher salt and freshly ground black pepper

Cod Sticks

Cooking spray

1 cup all-purpose flour

1 teaspoon smoked paprika

3 large eggs

2 cups panko bread crumbs

1/4 cup finely chopped fresh parsley

2 pounds cod fillets, cut into 1-inch-wide strips

1/2 teaspoon kosher salt

1/2 teaspoon freshly ground black pepper

Olive oil, for drizzling

Store-bought tartar sauce (optional)

Lemon wedges (optional)

SERVES 6 TO 8 I grew up eating and loving fish sticks. My mom used to buy them frozen (you know, the box with the fisherman in the bright yellow rain gear) and always paired them with peas and mashed potatoes. I still love fish sticks just as much now as I did back then, but these days I make them from scratch because they are so simple to make—and now that I have a grown-up palate, so much more flavorful than the frozen ones! Serve with dipping sauces and lemon wedges, and you've got a delicious update to a nostalgic favorite, although I still serve the same sides as Mom did. Sometimes I will enlist the kids at the dredging station to coat the fish, and this speeds things up a bit.

1. **MAKE THE BANG BANG SAUCE:** In a small bowl, stir together the mayonnaise, Thai chili sauce, and sriracha. Season with salt and pepper. Cover and refrigerate until ready to serve. (The sauce can be refrigerated for up to 1 day. Let come to room temperature before serving.)

2. **MAKE THE COD STICKS:** Preheat the oven to 400°F. Line a half-sheet pan with parchment paper. Mist the paper with cooking spray.

3. **SET UP A DREDGING STATION IN THREE SHALLOW BOWLS:** In the first bowl, mix the flour and smoked paprika. Beat the eggs in a second bowl. In the third bowl, mix the panko and parsley.

4. Season the cod all over with the salt and pepper. One at a time, coat the cod strips first in the flour, then in the eggs, and finally in the panko. Place on the prepared half-sheet pan. Drizzle the strips with olive oil.

5. Bake for 10 minutes. Carefully flip the strips and continue baking until golden brown, about 10 minutes more. Serve hot with the bang bang sauce, tartar sauce (if using), and lemon wedges (if using).

Dinner
Time!

How many times have you stood in front of your opened refrigerator at dinner time, just staring at the contents inside, willing the food to jump onto the counter and assemble itself into some delicious and satisfying meal? I have been there. The reasons for menu burnout are countless: frustration with picky eaters, feeling too exhausted after a busy day to even consider cooking or cleaning up, the pressure of preparing healthy meals. I could go on. But instead, let me lend you a hand. These are the recipes that my family loves.

Need a comforting meal to soothe after-work nerves? I've got you covered with nostalgic recipes (such as Chicken Divan and Sheet Pan Lasagna on pages 98 and 111), which are my versions of a deep-tissue massage. Do you want an impressive meal for guests? You'll find a wonderful seafood stew (see Cioppino, page 120), a gorgeous ham for your biggest party (page 129), and ideas for casual and impromptu gatherings.

Everyone (and I mean *everyone*) needs a collection of one-dish recipes, and you'll find several here. And then there is good old reliable pasta, whether Asian noodles such as Spicy Garlic Noodles with Shiitakes (page 153) or Rigatoni with Creamy Sausage Sauce (page 145) that would make my Italian grandma proud. In fact, some of the recipes are directly from her recipe box and are dishes the Montellis have been eating for generations!

Chicken Divan

Cooking spray

Kosher salt

2 pounds broccoli crowns, cut into florets

2 tablespoons vegetable oil, as needed

1½ pounds boneless, skinless chicken breasts, cut into bite-sized pieces (see Note)

Freshly ground black pepper

Sauce

5 tablespoons unsalted butter

½ cup all-purpose flour

3 cups chicken broth

2 cups whole milk

1 teaspoon Worcestershire sauce

2 teaspoons Dijon mustard

1 teaspoon garlic powder

1 teaspoon onion powder

2 cups shredded sharp cheddar cheese

Kosher salt and freshly ground black pepper

Topping

1½ cups panko bread crumbs or crushed flaky butter crackers (such as Ritz)

1 cup shredded sharp cheddar cheese

3 tablespoons unsalted butter, melted

2 garlic cloves, minced

Chopped fresh parsley, for garnish

Note

Save a step (step 3, literally) by substituting 3 to 4 cups bite-sized meat from a rotisserie chicken for the sautéed chicken.

SERVES 6 Back in the day, when all my friends were having babies, this is the dish I made them for when they returned home from the hospital because I knew how well this recipe would be welcomed, as it was comforting, nostalgic, and delicious. Also, while Mom was recuperating, the rest of the family would be well fed by this filling casserole. In the past, I made it with canned soup, but now I make my own from-scratch sauce.

1. Coat a 9 × 13-inch baking dish with cooking spray.

2. Bring a large pot of salted water to a boil over high heat. Add the broccoli and cook until it is crisp-tender and bright green, about 3 minutes. Drain and rinse under cold running water to stop the cooking. Pat dry with paper towels. Spread the broccoli in the baking dish.

3. Heat the oil in a large skillet over medium-high heat. Season the chicken with 1 teaspoon salt and ½ teaspoon pepper. Working in batches, add the chicken and cook, turning occasionally, until seared on all sides, about 8 minutes, adding more oil as needed. As it is cooked, scatter the chicken over the broccoli.

4. Preheat the oven to 400°F.

5. **MAKE THE SAUCE:** Melt the butter in a large saucepan over medium heat. Sprinkle in the flour and whisk until smooth. Whisking often, let the roux bubble without browning for about 2 minutes. Whisk in the broth, then the milk, increase the heat to medium-high, and bring to a simmer, whisking often. Reduce the heat to low and cook, still whisking often, until lightly thickened to soup consistency, about 3 minutes. Whisk in the Worcestershire sauce, mustard, garlic powder, and onion powder. Remove from the heat and whisk in the cheddar. Season with salt and pepper. Spread the sauce over the chicken and broccoli and stir lightly to combine.

6. **MAKE THE TOPPING:** In a small bowl, mix together the panko, cheddar, melted butter, and garlic. Sprinkle over the sauce.

7. Bake until the sauce is bubbling and the topping is golden brown, about 30 minutes. Sprinkle with the parsley and serve hot.

Chicken and Spinach Mac and Cheese

2 tablespoons vegetable oil

5 bacon slices

3 boneless, skinless chicken breasts (10 to 12 ounces each)

2 teaspoons smoked paprika

2 teaspoons Italian seasoning

Kosher salt and freshly ground black pepper

2 tablespoons unsalted butter

1 yellow onion, chopped

4 garlic cloves, chopped

2⅓ cups chicken broth

⅓ cup all-purpose flour

4 cups whole milk

1 tablespoon finely chopped fresh rosemary

¼ teaspoon crushed red pepper flakes

1 cup slivered oil-packed sun-dried tomatoes, drained

1 pound cavatappi or other tube-shaped pasta (such as ziti)

1 cup freshly grated Parmigiano-Reggiano cheese

1 cup shredded mozzarella cheese

1 cup shredded sharp cheddar cheese

3 cups baby spinach leaves

¼ cup finely chopped fresh parsley

SERVES 8 TO 10 This creamy stovetop macaroni and cheese is loaded with three different types of cheese and amped up more with chicken and crumbled bacon. The pasta also cooks directly in the sauce, not beforehand in a pot of water, which reduces the cooking time and makes the dish super rich, too. This recipe makes a lot, so be sure to use a large skillet or a wide heavy-bottomed saucepan.

1. Heat the oil in a heavy 5- to 6-quart saucepan or Dutch oven over medium heat. Add the bacon and cook, turning occasionally, until crisp and browned, about 7 minutes. Transfer the bacon to paper towels to drain and cool, leaving the drippings in the pan.

2. Pound the chicken to a ½-inch thickness (see Note). In a small bowl, mix together the smoked paprika, 1 teaspoon of the Italian seasoning, 1 teaspoon salt, and ½ teaspoon pepper. Season the chicken with the paprika mixture.

3. Add the chicken to the saucepan with the bacon drippings and cook over medium-high heat until the underside is browned, about 4 minutes. Flip the chicken and cook until the other side is browned and the chicken shows no sign of pink when pierced in the center with the tip of a small knife, about 4 minutes more. Transfer the chicken to a plate.

4. Add the butter to the saucepan and let it melt. Add the onion and garlic and cook over medium heat, stirring often, until the onion begins to soften, about 2 minutes. Add ⅓ cup of the broth and cook until the broth has almost completely reduced, 2 to 3 minutes. Sprinkle in the flour, stir well, and let the mixture cook without browning, about 1 minute. Whisk in the milk, the remaining 2 cups broth, rosemary, pepper flakes, and remaining 1 teaspoon Italian seasoning. Bring to a simmer, whisking often. Stir in the sun-dried tomatoes. Reduce the heat to medium-low and simmer, whisking often, until lightly thickened, about 5 minutes.

Note

Pounding the chicken breast halves to give them even thickness will allow them to cook at the same rate. One at a time, place a chicken breast half between two sheets of plastic wrap or slip it inside of a 1-gallon resealable plastic bag. Using a flat meat pounder or a rolling pin, pound the chicken so it is about 1/2 inch thick.

5. Stir in the pasta, increase the heat to medium, and bring to a simmer. Return the heat to medium-low and simmer, stirring often, until the pasta is barely tender, 8 to 10 minutes. Add the Parmigiano, mozzarella, and cheddar and stir until melted. Stir in the spinach and cook until wilted, about 1 minute. Season with salt and black pepper.

6. Remove from the heat. Cut the chicken into bite-sized pieces and add to the saucepan. Crumble the bacon and add to the saucepan, along with the parsley. Stir well and serve hot.

Turkey Pesto Meatballs with Roasted Pepper Sauce

Meatballs

2 pounds ground turkey or chicken (not white meat only)

1½ cups panko bread crumbs

½ cup pesto

½ cup freshly grated Parmigiano-Reggiano cheese

2 large eggs, lightly beaten

¼ cup finely chopped fresh parsley

1 shallot, grated on the large holes of a box grater

Finely grated zest of 1 lemon

1 tablespoon dried oregano

1 teaspoon garlic powder

1 teaspoon kosher salt

½ teaspoon freshly ground black pepper

Pinch of crushed red pepper flakes

Cooking spray, preferably olive oil

Creamy Roasted Pepper Sauce

1 24-ounce jar roasted red peppers, drained

3 tablespoons olive oil

1 shallot, finely chopped

4 garlic cloves, thinly sliced

½ teaspoon Italian seasoning

½ teaspoon crushed red pepper flakes

½ teaspoon kosher salt, plus more to taste

½ teaspoon freshly ground black pepper

1 cup heavy cream

5 fresh basil leaves, torn into small pieces

1 pound ziti or rigatoni

Freshly grated Parmigiano-Reggiano cheese, for serving

SERVES 6 TO 8 Although my mom's meatball game was legendary, she never veered from her recipe. But meatballs are versatile because they can be made with nearly any type of meat, and seasonings. The secret to these juicy meatballs is pesto, which lends its signature flavor and pretty green hue while also providing extra moisture, a plus for lean ground poultry. While this recipe is for a main course in a roasted pepper sauce (here, over pasta, but rice or polenta is good, too), you can also simmer the meatballs in soup, serve them on a salad, skewer mini meatballs on toothpicks as an appetizer with a dipping sauce, or stuff them into a submarine roll.

1. **MAKE THE MEATBALLS:** In a large bowl, combine the ground turkey, panko, pesto, and Parmigiano and mix lightly with clean, just-rinsed, wet hands. Add the eggs, parsley, shallot, lemon zest, oregano, garlic powder, salt, black pepper, and pepper flakes and mix well to combine. Cover and refrigerate for 30 minutes to firm up the mixture.

2. Line a half-sheet pan with parchment paper or foil and spritz with cooking spray. Using wet, rinsed hands, roll the mixture in balls about 2 inches in diameter and place on the prepared pan. Refrigerate for 30 minutes to 1 hour.

3. Preheat the oven to 375°F.

4. **MEANWHILE, MAKE THE CREAMY ROASTED PEPPER SAUCE:** In a blender or food processor, puree the peppers. Heat the oil in a large saucepan over medium heat. Add the shallot and cook, stirring often, until softened, about 2 minutes. Add the garlic and stir occasionally until it is softened and fragrant, about 1 minute more. Stir in the roasted pepper puree, Italian seasoning, pepper flakes, salt, and black pepper. Bring to a boil over high heat. Return the heat to medium and cook at a brisk simmer, stirring often to avoid scorching, until slightly reduced, about 10 minutes.

Continues

5. With an immersion blender, blend the sauce until smooth. Stir in the cream and basil and bring to a simmer. Season with additional salt, if needed.

6. Meanwhile, spray the meatballs with olive oil. Bake until beginning to brown, about 20 minutes.

7. Add the meatballs to the sauce and bring to a simmer over medium-high heat. Reduce the heat to medium-low and simmer, covered, until the meatballs are cooked through and the sauce has reduced slightly, about 30 minutes.

8. Bring a large pot of salted water to a boil over high heat. Add the ziti and cook according to the package directions until tender. Drain and transfer to a bowl or deep serving platter.

9. Pour the sauce and meatballs over the ziti and serve hot, with the Parmigiano on the side.

Chicken and Vegetable Shepherd's Pie

Mashed Potato Topping

2½ pounds baking potatoes (such as russet or Idaho), peeled and cut into chunks

Kosher salt

¼ cup sour cream

5 tablespoons unsalted butter, sliced

¼ cup whole milk

Filling

5 tablespoons unsalted butter

1 yellow onion, chopped

1 celery rib, chopped

4 garlic cloves, finely chopped

⅓ cup all-purpose flour

2 cups whole milk

2 cups reduced-sodium chicken broth

1 tablespoon finely chopped fresh thyme

4 cups shredded or diced cooked chicken (rotisserie chicken is fine)

3 cups frozen mixed peas and carrots, thawed

1½ cups frozen pearl onions, thawed

1 teaspoon Worcestershire sauce

Pinch of cayenne pepper

Kosher salt and freshly ground black pepper

3 tablespoons freshly grated Parmigiano-Reggiano cheese

2 tablespoons chopped fresh parsley, for garnish

SERVES 6 TO 8   When I was growing up, one of our family dinner favorites was cottage pie with ground beef under a mashed potato topping. Sometimes, Mom would make a lighter, chicken version from a freshly braised chicken. Nowadays, I make this with chicken, but I'm more likely to use rotisserie chicken meat. Let's not have an argument about whether this is a shepherd's pie (made with lamb) or should instead be called a "cottage pie" (because it is not). No matter what you call it, it is always good and especially nice on a chilly night.

1. Preheat the oven to 400°F. Lightly oil a 9 × 13-inch baking dish.

2. **MAKE THE MASHED POTATO TOPPING:** In a large saucepan, combine the potatoes with enough cold salted water to cover them by 1 inch. Bring to a boil over high heat. Reduce the heat to medium-low and simmer until the potatoes are tender when pierced with a small knife, about 20 minutes.

3. Drain the potatoes and return them to the saucepan. Add the sour cream, butter, and milk and mash well with a potato masher. Season with salt. Cover to keep warm and set aside.

4. **MEANWHILE, MAKE THE FILLING:** Melt the butter in another large saucepan over medium heat. Add the onion, celery, and garlic and cook, stirring often, until the vegetables are tender, about 5 minutes. Sprinkle in the flour and stir well. Cook, stirring often, about 1 minute. Gradually stir in the milk and broth, followed by the thyme. Increase the heat to high and bring to a boil, stirring often. Reduce the heat to medium-low and simmer, stirring often, until the sauce is lightly thickened, about 3 minutes.

5. Stir in the chicken, peas and carrots, pearl onions, Worcestershire, and cayenne. Season with salt and black pepper. Spread the filling in the prepared baking dish. Spoon the mashed potatoes on top and spread as evenly as possible. Sprinkle with the Parmigiano.

6. Bake until the topping is lightly browned and the sauce is bubbling, 30 to 40 minutes. Sprinkle with the parsley and serve hot.

Seafood-Stuffed Portobellos

Olive oil, for the pan

6 portobello mushrooms, about 2½ inches in diameter

¼ cup olive oil

½ small onion, chopped

3 garlic cloves, minced

8 ounces peeled and deveined shrimp, finely chopped

8 ounces sea or bay scallops, finely chopped

2 cups crushed flaky butter crackers, such as Ritz

½ cup freshly grated Parmigiano-Reggiano cheese

½ cup mayonnaise

2 tablespoons finely chopped fresh basil

2 tablespoons finely chopped fresh parsley, plus more for garnish

2 teaspoons finely chopped fresh rosemary

Kosher salt and freshly ground black pepper

Lemon wedges, for squeezing

SERVES 6 Big portobello mushrooms, with a dense, meaty texture that stands up well to baking, beg to be stuffed. They are the perfect vessels for just about any filling you can dream of, and this seafood version is one of the best. The filling bakes to a beautiful golden brown while the mushroom remains juicy and tender.

1. Preheat the oven to 350°F. Lightly coat a half-sheet pan with olive oil.

2. Wipe the portobellos clean with a damp paper towel. Snap off the stems and save for another use, such as soup or stock. Using a teaspoon, gently scrape out and discard the black gills from each portobello cap.

3. Heat the ¼ cup oil in a large skillet over medium-high heat. Add the onion and garlic and cook, stirring often, until the onions are softened, about 3 minutes. Add the shrimp and scallops and cook, stirring often, just until they turn opaque, about 2 minutes. Be careful not to overcook them or they will be dense and chewy.

4. Transfer the mixture to a bowl. Add the crackers, Parmigiano, mayonnaise, basil, parsley, and rosemary and stir to combine. Season with salt and pepper.

5. Arrange the mushroom caps, scraped-side up, on the half-sheet pan. Divide the seafood filling among the caps, pressing to slightly compact each into a mound.

6. Bake until the filling is lightly browned, about 30 minutes. Sprinkle with parsley and serve hot, with lemon wedges for squeezing.

VARIATION

Crab and Cod Stuffed Mushrooms: Substitute 8 ounces crabmeat (picked over for shells and cartilage) for the shrimp. Substitute 8 ounces cod fillet, finely chopped, for the scallops.

Sheet Pan Lasagna

Béchamel

4 tablespoons (½ stick) unsalted butter

¼ cup all-purpose flour

2 cups whole milk

Kosher salt and freshly ground black pepper

Ricotta Topping

1½ cups whole-milk or part-skim ricotta cheese

¼ cup shredded low-moisture mozzarella cheese

¼ cup freshly grated Parmigiano-Reggiano cheese

1 large egg, lightly beaten

¼ cup chopped fresh parsley

½ teaspoon crushed red pepper flakes

¼ teaspoon garlic powder

Beef and Spinach Sauce

2 tablespoons olive oil

10 ounces white or cremini mushrooms, thinly sliced

1 yellow onion, chopped

3 garlic cloves, finely chopped

1 pound lean ground beef (90% lean)

1 teaspoon kosher salt

5 cups Marinara Sauce, homemade (page 126) or store-bought

1 5-ounce bag baby spinach

SERVES 9   This lasagna is assembled with most of the actual components found in my traditional lasagna but without the tedious layering process, plus I use a bonus of creamy béchamel sauce to make it even more over-the-top. The components (except for the pasta) can be made ahead, and it cooks in less time than the "big" version. It's a fun spin on a classic recipe and a perfect dish to feed a crowd. Put out some garlic bread and a big salad to go with it.

1. **MAKE THE BÉCHAMEL:** Melt the butter in a medium saucepan over medium heat. Whisk in the flour and let it bubble without browning for 2 minutes. Gradually whisk in the milk and bring to a boil. Reduce the heat to medium-low and simmer, whisking often, until thickened, about 3 minutes. Season with salt and pepper. (The béchamel can be cooled and refrigerated in a covered container for up to 1 day. Reheat in a saucepan over medium heat, whisking often, until warmed and spreadable.)

2. **MAKE THE RICOTTA TOPPING:** In a medium bowl, stir together the ricotta, mozzarella, Parmigiano, egg, parsley, pepper flakes, and garlic powder. (The topping can be refrigerated in a covered container for up to 1 day.)

3. **MAKE THE BEEF AND SPINACH SAUCE:** Heat the oil in a large Dutch oven over medium-high heat. Add the mushrooms, onion, and garlic and cook, stirring often, until the mushrooms give off their juices, about 5 minutes.

4. Add the ground beef and cook, stirring occasionally and breaking up the beef with the side of a spoon, until it loses its raw look, about 8 minutes. Sprinkle in the salt.

5. Stir in the marinara sauce and bring to a simmer. A handful at a time, stir in the spinach, letting each addition wilt before adding another. Remove from the heat. (The filling can be cooled and refrigerated in a covered container for up to 1 day.)

Continues

Assembly

Cooking spray

Kosher salt

1 pound mafaldine pasta (see Note), broken into 3-inch lengths

1½ cups freshly grated Parmigiano-Reggiano cheese

1½ cups shredded low-moisture mozzarella cheese

Note

Mafaldine pasta looks like thin ribbons of lasagna noodles. These are easier to eat than the wide noodles. If you can't find it, substitute 1 pound standard lasagna noodles, broken up into 2- to 3-inch lengths.

6. **TO ASSEMBLE:** Preheat the oven to 400°F. Mist a half-sheet pan with the spray.

7. Bring a large pot of salted water to a boil over high heat. Add the pasta and cook, stirring occasionally, until just al dente according to the package directions. Scoop out and reserve ½ cup of the pasta cooking water. Drain the pasta. Add the pasta, reserved pasta water, and ½ cup of the Parmigiano to the beef sauce.

8. Spread the beef sauce/pasta mixture evenly onto the pan—the pan will be full. Spoon the béchamel sauce over the pasta and swirl it in with a dinner knife. Space 9 big dollops of the ricotta topping evenly over the béchamel. Sprinkle with the mozzarella and the remaining 1 cup Parmigiano.

9. Bake until the sauce is bubbling and the topping is golden brown, about 30 minutes. (While it has never happened to me, if you are concerned about the lasagna boiling over into your oven, line the oven rack under the pan with aluminum foil to catch any drips.)

10. Let stand for 5 minutes. Cut into individual servings and serve with a wide spatula, being sure each serving has a ricotta dollop on top.

Classic Meatloaf with Diner Gravy

Meatloaf

Cooking spray

2 pounds ground round (85% lean)

1 cup panko bread crumbs

1 small yellow onion, finely chopped

1 carrot, shredded

2 garlic cloves, minced

1/2 cup whole milk

2/3 cup ketchup

2 large eggs, lightly beaten

1 tablespoon Worcestershire sauce

1 tablespoon Dijon mustard

2 tablespoons finely chopped fresh parsley

1 1/2 teaspoons kosher salt

1/2 teaspoon garlic powder

1/4 teaspoon freshly ground black pepper

Gravy

3 tablespoons unsalted butter

1/4 cup all-purpose flour

1 3/4 cups reduced-sodium beef broth

1 teaspoon reduced-sodium soy sauce

Kosher salt and freshly ground black pepper

SERVES 6 For a dinner that pushes all the comfort food buttons, you can't beat meatloaf and gravy with mashed potatoes. Traditional and comforting, easy and economical, you might find it worthwhile to double the recipe and make two loaves to have leftovers for meatloaf sandwiches. Mom always made the BBQ glaze version (see page 114), in which case you may not want the gravy.

1. Preheat the oven to 350°F. Lightly coat a 9 × 13-inch metal baking pan with the cooking spray.

2. **MAKE THE MEATLOAF:** In a large bowl, combine the ground round, panko, onion, carrot, garlic, milk, 1/3 cup of the ketchup, the eggs, Worcestershire sauce, mustard, parsley, salt, garlic powder, and pepper and mix with clean, just-rinsed, wet hands. Do not overmix or the meatloaf could be tough.

3. Dump the mixture onto the prepared pan and shape with rinsed, wet hands into a free-form loaf about 9 × 5 inches.

4. Bake until an instant-read thermometer inserted in the center reads at least 165°F, about 1 hour. During the last 10 minutes, spread with the remaining 1/3 cup ketchup.

5. Remove from the oven. Let stand for 5 minutes. Using a pancake turner or large spatula, transfer the meatloaf to a platter, reserving the pan and the drippings. Tent the meatloaf with aluminum foil to keep warm.

6. **MAKE THE GRAVY:** Add the butter to the drippings in the baking pan. Heat over medium heat to melt the butter. Whisk in the flour, whisking up the browned bits in the baking dish. Cook until lightly browned, about 2 minutes. Whisk in the broth, 3/4 cup water, and soy sauce, scraping up the browned bits in the pan, and bring to a simmer. Cook, whisking often, until thickened, about 3 minutes. Season with salt and pepper.

7. Slice the meatloaf and serve with the gravy.

Continues

GRILLED BBQ MEATLOAF AND CHEDDAR SANDWICHES

Makes 1 sandwich

1 thick slice meatloaf

1 kaiser roll, split

2 slices sharp cheddar cheese

Barbecue sauce or BBQ glaze

1 slice beefsteak tomato

1 red lettuce leaf

Caramelized Onions (page 84; optional) or frozen onion rings from the supermarket reheated in the toaster oven or air fryer

Here's the meatloaf sandwich that my family loves. It's kinda sorta an upgraded cheeseburger. Mix up some BBQ glaze (in a small bowl, whisk 2/3 cup ketchup, 2 tablespoons brown sugar, and 2 tablespoons cider vinegar), if you wish, for a condiment.

1. Warm the meatloaf in the microwave oven. Place the kaiser roll, cut-side up, on a broiler pan. Put the meatloaf on the bottom half, and top the cheese. Broil on high until the cheese melts and the top of the roll is toasted. Spread the roll top with barbecue sauce. Add the tomato and lettuce (and some caramelized onions, if you have them). Cap with the roll top, cut in half, and serve.

Seared Salmon with Orange-Avocado Salad

Salmon

2 tablespoons vegetable or canola oil

4 salmon fillets (6 ounces each), skinned

Kosher salt and freshly ground black pepper

Finely grated zest of 1 navel orange

1/2 cup fresh orange juice

1/4 cup honey

1/4 cup soy sauce

2 tablespoons grated fresh ginger, grated on a Microplane

3 garlic cloves, grated on a Microplane

1/4 teaspoon crushed red pepper flakes

Salad

1/3 cup Miso-Carrot Dressing (recipe follows), or more as desired

5 ounces baby greens

2 navel oranges, peeled, cut into 1/4-inch-thick rounds, and seeded

2 blood (such as Moro) or navel (such as Cara Cara) oranges, peeled and cut into 1/4-inch-thick rounds, and seeded

2 Hass avocados, cut lengthwise into 1/4-inch slices

2 tablespoons finely chopped fresh chives

SERVES 4 Searing salmon in a hot skillet locks in the natural juices and heart-healthy oils while creating an irresistible golden crust. This simple technique provides the biggest return on flavor. Served over a simple salad, which includes sliced oranges and avocado to keep things bright and healthy, you have a dinner that is both gorgeous and flavorful. When I make it for company, I use two different kinds of oranges, but since this is also a great dinner that my family loves, I might even swap in grapefruit. It's a dish for all occasions and all seasons.

1. **COOK THE SALMON:** Heat the oil in a large nonstick skillet over medium-high heat. Season the salmon with 1/2 teaspoon salt and 1/4 teaspoon pepper. Place the salmon, flesh-side down, in the skillet and cook, without disturbing, until the underside is golden brown, about 4 minutes. Flip the salmon over and cook to lightly brown the skinned side, about 3 minutes. Transfer to a platter and tent with foil to keep warm.

2. Meanwhile, in a small bowl, whisk together the orange zest, orange juice, honey, soy sauce, ginger, garlic, and pepper flakes.

3. Return the skillet to high heat. Add the orange juice mixture and bring to a boil. Boil, stirring occasionally, until the mixture is reduced by half, about 3 minutes. Return the salmon to the skillet, skinned-side down, and cook until the sauce is syrupy, about 1 minute. Season with salt and pepper. Remove from the heat.

4. **ASSEMBLE THE SALAD:** Toss the greens with the dressing. Divide the greens among four dinner plates. Assemble the orange and avocado slices over the greens. Top each with a salmon fillet, drizzle with the sauce from the skillet, sprinkle with the chives, and serve.

MISO-CARROT DRESSING

Makes about 1½ cups

2 medium carrots (about 5 ounces), peeled and coarsely chopped

¼ cup unseasoned rice vinegar

3 tablespoons white (shiro) miso

1-inch piece fresh ginger, peeled and cut into thin rounds

2 tablespoons fresh lime juice

2 tablespoons grapeseed or vegetable oil

1 tablespoon toasted sesame oil

1½ teaspoons sugar

Kosher salt and freshly ground black pepper

Get in the habit of making this dressing to have on hand for salads and more (we like it, on the thick side, as a veggie dip, too).

In a blender (preferably heavy-duty), combine the carrots, vinegar, miso, ginger, lime juice, grapeseed oil, sesame oil, and sugar and process to make a coarse puree. If you like a thinner dressing, blend in water, a tablespoon at a time, to get the desired consistency. Season with salt and pepper. (Transfer the dressing to a covered container and refrigerate for up to 5 days. Stir well before using.)

Spicy Butter Shrimp on Creamy Corn Polenta

Creamy Corn Polenta

3½ cups reduced-sodium chicken broth

½ cup heavy cream

1 teaspoon kosher salt

1 cup polenta (coarse yellow cornmeal)

3 cups corn kernels, fresh (from 3 to 4 ears) or thawed frozen

½ cup freshly grated Parmigiano-Reggiano cheese

3 tablespoons unsalted butter

½ teaspoon freshly ground black pepper

Spicy Butter Shrimp

1½ pounds large (21/25 count) shrimp, peeled and deveined, tails left on

2 teaspoons Cajun seasoning

1 stick (4 ounces) unsalted butter

2 garlic cloves, finely chopped

Finely grated zest and juice of 1 lemon

1 tablespoon Worcestershire sauce

1 tablespoon finely chopped fresh thyme

Kosher salt and freshly ground black pepper

SERVES 4 TO 6 This spicy shrimp over creamy polenta is perfectly spiced and full of smoky flavor. The great thing is that the spice levels can be adjusted depending on how much heat you like. If you want it spicier, add a little more cayenne; less spicy, hold back on the seasoning. Don't sleep on polenta as a side dish—it's as good as any risotto or pasta you can come up with.

1. **MAKE THE CREAMY CORN POLENTA:** In a medium saucepan, combine the broth, cream, and salt. Bring to a boil over high heat. Gradually whisk in the polenta and return to a boil. Reduce the heat to medium-low and cook, whisking often, until the polenta is thick, about 10 minutes.

2. Stir in the corn kernels and continue cooking, whisking often, until the polenta is tender and smooth, about 10 minutes more. Add the Parmigiano, butter, and pepper and whisk to combine. Cover tightly and keep warm over very low heat.

3. **MEANWHILE, PREPARE THE SPICY BUTTER SHRIMP:** In a bowl, toss together the shrimp and Cajun seasoning. Let stand at room temperature for about 10 minutes.

4. Melt the butter in a large skillet over medium-high heat. Add the shrimp and spread in a single layer. Cook until the shrimp edges turn opaque, 1 to 2 minutes. Flip the shrimp over and continue cooking until the shrimp is opaque throughout, about 2 minutes more. Add the garlic and cook until fragrant, about 30 seconds. Stir in the lemon zest, lemon juice, Worcestershire sauce, and thyme. Season with salt and pepper.

5. Spoon the hot polenta into bowls, top with the shrimp and its sauce, and serve.

Cioppino

1/4 cup olive oil

3 oil-packed anchovy fillets, chopped

1 teaspoon crushed red pepper flakes

6 garlic cloves, finely chopped

1 bay leaf

1 yellow onion, chopped

3 celery ribs, chopped

1/4 cup tomato paste

1 cup dry white wine

1 28-ounce can crushed tomatoes

2 cups bottled clam juice

4 fresh thyme sprigs

2 pounds cod, scrod, or haddock fillets

Kosher salt and freshly ground black pepper

2 dozen fresh mussels, cleaned (see Note)

2 dozen fresh littleneck clams, cleaned (see Note)

1 pound large (21/25 count) shrimp, peeled and deveined

1 pound sea scallops

1/3 cup finely chopped fresh parsley

Note

To clean the clams and mussels, scrub them well under cold running water. If the mussels have their beards, pull them off with your hands or a pair of pliers. (Prince Edward Island mussels, a common variety, are beardless.) Transfer the clams and mussels to a large bowl of well-salted cold water and let stand for 30 minutes. Drain well before adding to the broth.

SERVES 6 TO 8 Cioppino is a fisherman's stew popularized in San Francisco, with a robust red broth and chock-full of seafood. I make a pot of this every Christmas Eve because the broth can be made the day before and refrigerated. When you are ready to serve it, bring it to a simmer and add the seafood, then serve it up with plenty of crusty bread to soak up all that flavorful broth.

1. Heat the oil in a large pot over medium heat. Add the anchovies, pepper flakes, garlic, and bay leaf and cook, stirring often, until the anchovies begin to break down, about 1 minute. Add the onion and celery and cook, stirring often, until softened, about 3 minutes. Stir the tomato paste into the vegetables and continue to cook until the tomato paste begins to brown and to stick to the bottom of the pot, 2 to 3 minutes. Add the wine and scrape up the tomato paste with a wooden spoon.

2. Add the crushed tomatoes, clam juice, and thyme. Increase the heat to high and bring to a boil. Reduce the heat to medium-low and simmer to blend the flavors, about 10 minutes. Remove and discard the thyme stems and the bay leaf. (The broth can be cooled, covered, and refrigerated for up to 1 day. Bring to a simmer over high heat before proceeding.)

3. Season the cod with 1/2 teaspoon salt and 1/4 teaspoon pepper. Add to the broth and cook, without stirring, for 5 minutes. Add the mussels, clams, shrimp, and scallops and cover tightly. Simmer until the mussels and clams open, about 10 minutes. Discard any unopened clams or mussels.

4. Season the broth with salt and pepper. Sprinkle in the parsley. Ladle into bowls, breaking up the cod as needed to fit the bowls, and serve hot.

Grilled Chile-Lime Flank Steak with Grilled Pineapple Salsa

Marinated Flank Steak

3 tablespoons extra-virgin olive oil

3 tablespoons fresh lime juice

1 teaspoon chili powder

1 teaspoon kosher salt

1/2 teaspoon ground cumin

1/2 teaspoon smoked paprika

1/2 teaspoon garlic powder

1/2 teaspoon freshly ground black pepper

2 pounds flank steak

Grilled Pineapple Salsa

1 large pineapple, peeled and cut crosswise into 1/2-inch-thick rounds

1 red bell pepper, halved lengthwise and seeded

1 jalapeño pepper, halved lengthwise and seeded

1 lime, halved

2 tablespoons olive oil, plus more for brushing

1 teaspoon honey

1/2 teaspoon ground cumin

1/2 teaspoon kosher salt

1/4 teaspoon freshly ground black pepper

1/2 cup chopped red onion

2 tablespoons chopped fresh cilantro

SERVES 6 Marinated flank steak, grilled to perfection and served with a bright and vibrant salsa, is a classic recipe that everyone will love and that will quickly be added to your dinner rotation. The pineapple for the salsa caramelizes as it grills making it incredibly flavorful and juicy. I especially love this salsa because it's so versatile. It is also amazing on grilled marinated chicken or shrimp, which you can throw on the grill for those who don't eat meat. If using chicken, marinate for up to 4 hours, but marinate shrimp for no longer than 1 hour. Serve it all from a large platter as is, or add a big stack of warmed small "street taco" tortillas so everyone can make tacos.

1. **MARINATE THE STEAK:** In a small bowl, mix together the oil, lime juice, chili powder, salt, cumin, paprika, garlic powder, and pepper. Spread the paste over both sides of the steak in a glass baking dish. Cover with plastic wrap. Let stand at room temperature for up to 2 hours or refrigerate for up to 4 hours.

2. **MAKE THE SALSA:** Preheat a gas grill to high. For a charcoal fire, let the coals burn until they are covered with white ash and you can barely hold your hand just above the cooking grate for 2 seconds. Brush the grate clean.

3. Brush the pineapple rounds, the skin sides of the bell pepper and jalapeño, and cut sides of the lime with oil. Grill the pineapple until the underside is seared with grill marks, about 6 minutes. Flip the pineapple and sear the other side, about 6 minutes more. Transfer to a cutting board. Add the bell pepper, jalapeño, and lime halves to the grill, oiled-side down, and cook until seared with grill marks, about 3 minutes. Remove the lime halves and set aside to cool. Flip the bell pepper and jalapeño halves, and continue grilling until softened, about 3 minutes more. Transfer the pepper and jalapeño to the cutting board. Let the pineapple, pepper, and jalapeño stand until cool enough to handle.

Continues

4. Use a large knife to chop the pineapple, discarding the cores, and transfer to a large bowl. Chop the bell pepper and jalapeño a little smaller than the pineapple and add to the bowl.

5. Squeeze the juice from the grilled lime halves into a small bowl. Add the 2 tablespoons oil, the honey, cumin, salt, and pepper and whisk to combine.

6. Pour the lime mixture over the pineapple mixture and mix well. Stir in the red onion and cilantro. Let stand at room temperature for 30 minutes to 1 hour to blend the flavors.

7. GRILL THE STEAK: When ready to cook the steak, preheat a gas grill on high. If you are using a charcoal grill, add more briquettes or wood to the grill and let burn until covered with white ash. For either a gas or charcoal grill, brush the grill grates clean. Place the steak on the grill and close the lid. Grill until the underside is well browned, about 4 minutes. Flip the steak and grill until browned on the other side and an instant-read thermometer inserted in the center reads 125°F for medium-rare steak, 3 to 4 minutes more.

8. Transfer to a carving board, tent with aluminum foil, and let stand for 5 minutes.

9. Using a sharp thin knife held at a slight angle to the cutting board, cut the steak across the grain into ½-inch-thick slices. Serve hot with the salsa.

Note

The steak and salsa can also be cooked indoors on a grill pan. Heat a ridged grill pan or cast-iron skillet over medium-high heat. Follow the recipe timings.

Grandma's Braciole

2 to 2½ pounds beef top sirloin roast (see Note)

Kosher salt and freshly ground black pepper

1 cup freshly grated Parmigiano-Reggiano cheese, plus more for serving

1 small yellow onion, finely chopped

¼ cup minced fresh parsley, plus more for garnish

4 tablespoons olive oil

4 garlic cloves, chopped

1 teaspoon crushed red pepper flakes

5 cups Marinara Sauce, homemade (page 126) or store-bought

½ cup hearty red wine, such as Chianti

1½ pounds tube-shaped pasta, such as ziti or rigatoni

Note

Some butchers sell pre-sliced beef for braciole. Even if they do not, it is worth a shot to ask your butcher if they will slice the roast for you. If you have to slice the roast at home, it is easier to do if the meat is frozen for an hour or two before cutting with a thin, sharp carving knife.

SERVES 4 TO 6 This dish reminds me of Sundays with Grandma, the house filled with the aroma of simmering "Sunday sauce" made for her braciole, beef roulades with savory filling. This is the first recipe Grandma taught me, and everyone in my house loves it. We have an important family tradition when making them. I always use *exactly* three toothpicks per roulade. This came about because once I ate one of the toothpicks at Grandma's table. Since then, we use three so that everyone can count out the toothpicks—I always tell everyone "Make sure you remove *all three toothpicks* from your braciole!" to avoid another swallowing-toothpick episode. Serve over pasta so you don't miss one drop of the sauce.

1. Using a thin, sharp knife, cut the roast across the grain into 12 slices. One at a time, place between sheets of plastic wrap and pound with a flat meat pounder or rolling pin until ¼ inch thick. Mix 1 teaspoon salt and ½ teaspoon pepper in a small bowl. Season the beef slices on both sides with the salt mixture.

2. In a small bowl, combine the Parmigiano, onion, parsley, 2 tablespoons of the oil, the garlic, and pepper flakes. Sprinkle an equal amount of the cheese mixture in the center of each fillet and press it down to adhere to the meat. Starting from a short end, roll up each slice and close it with 3 toothpicks (or tie closed with kitchen twine).

3. Bring the marinara sauce to a simmer in a large Dutch oven over medium heat. Reduce the heat to low.

4. Heat the remaining 2 tablespoons oil in a large skillet over medium-high heat. Working in batches to avoid crowding, add the braciole and cook, turning occasionally, until browned on all sides, about 5 minutes. Transfer to a plate.

5. Add the red wine to the skillet and bring to a boil, scraping up the browned bits, to deglaze the skillet. Stir the wine into the sauce. Add the braciole to the sauce and adjust the heat so the sauce is simmering. Cover and simmer until the braciole are tender, about 1 hour.

Continues

6. Bring a large pot of salted water to a boil over high heat. Add the pasta and cook to al dente according to the package directions. Drain well and put in a large, deep bowl or platter.

7. Spoon about half of the sauce over the pasta and place the braciole on top. Spoon the remaining sauce over all. Sprinkle with parsley and serve hot. Pass grated Parmigiano at the table. Be sure to remind everyone to remove their toothpicks!

MARINARA SAUCE

Makes 5 cups

3 tablespoons olive oil

2 garlic cloves, chopped

2 28-ounce cans crushed tomatoes

Kosher salt and freshly ground black pepper

In the Italian American kitchen, there are two kinds of sauce: A Sunday gravy, which is made on the weekend when there's time to simmer it with lots of meat or braciole. And then there's this simple marinara sauce for everyday cooking, which everyone needs to know how to make practically without thinking.

Heat the oil and garlic in a large saucepan over medium heat and cook, stirring often, until the garlic is fragrant but not browned, about 2 minutes. Stir in the tomatoes and 1½ cups water. Bring to a boil over high heat. Reduce the heat to medium-low. Cook at a steady simmer, stirring often, until reduced to 5 cups, around 20 minutes.

Raspberry-Chipotle Baked Ham

1 14- to 16-pound fully cooked, spiral-cut smoked ham

1 18-ounce jar raspberry jam (1½ cups)

½ cup packed light brown sugar

3 tablespoons Dijon mustard

2 tablespoons balsamic vinegar

3 canned chipotle peppers in adobo sauce, finely chopped

2 tablespoons adobo sauce from the canned chipotles

3 garlic cloves, finely chopped

1 teaspoon smoked paprika

½ teaspoon cayenne pepper

SERVES ABOUT 20 My holiday parties always have a crowd, but I've got it down. One trick is to choose a main course that will easily feed a lot of people, can be served warm or at room temperature, and pairs well with many side dishes. And so that's why this ham is always going to be a favorite. Added bonuses: It's almost effortless to assemble and I can count on using any leftovers in so many different ways—sandwiches, omelets, stews, quiches, salads, or Ham, Cheese, and Chive Muffins (page 43). This glaze is a perfect combination of fruity, sweet, and spicy.

1. Preheat the oven to 325°F. Line a heavy roasting pan with parchment paper or aluminum foil.

2. Place the ham flat-side down in the roasting pan.

3. In a medium saucepan, combine the jam, brown sugar, mustard, vinegar, chipotles, adobo sauce, garlic, smoked paprika, and cayenne. Bring to a simmer over medium heat, stirring often to help melt the jam. Reduce the heat to low and simmer, stirring often, until the mixture thickens into a glaze, about 10 minutes.

4. Generously brush half of the glaze over the ham. Slide into the oven and bake for 1 hour. Remove from the oven and brush with the remaining glaze. Continue baking, until the ham is heated through (it should read 140°F on a meat thermometer) and the glaze is well browned, about 1 hour more. If the ham is browning too much, tent it with aluminum foil.

5. Remove from the oven and tent with foil until ready to serve. Serve warm or at room temperature.

Baked Buffalo Chicken Ranch Flautas

Dip

1 cup Ranch Dressing, homemade (page 131) or store-bought

3 tablespoons Buffalo wing sauce, such as Frank's

Pinch of kosher salt

Chicken Filling

4 cups shredded rotisserie chicken

2 cups shredded cheddar cheese

8 ounces cream cheese, at room temperature

½ cup crumbled blue cheese

½ cup Buffalo wing sauce, such as Frank's

¼ cup Ranch Dressing, homemade (recipe follows) or store-bought

4 scallions, white and green parts, chopped

3 tablespoons finely chopped fresh cilantro

Flautas

Cooking spray, preferably avocado

16 6-inch flour tortillas

Olive oil, for drizzling

1 scallion, white and green parts, chopped, for garnish

SERVES 8 My kids love Buffalo-flavored anything. These totally inauthentic flautas are one of my favorites, too, because they are delicious and a quick dish to throw together. The trick is using pulled rotisserie chicken. They are also good with barbecue sauce standing in for the ranch dressing. The great thing is that the filling can be made up to 2 days before, so they are just as perfect for entertaining as they are for a dinner-in-a-snap. Serve them with celery and carrot sticks and lots of the dip.

1. **MAKE THE DIP:** In a small bowl, whisk together the ranch dressing, Buffalo wing sauce, and salt.

2. **MAKE THE CHICKEN FILLING:** In a stand mixer fitted with the paddle, combine the chicken, cheddar, cream cheese, blue cheese, Buffalo wing sauce, ranch dressing, scallions, and cilantro. Mix until well combined. (The filling can be transferred to a 1-gallon resealable plastic bag and refrigerated for up to 2 days.)

3. **MAKE THE FLAUTAS:** Preheat the oven to 425°F. Spray a 10 × 15-inch baking pan with cooking spray.

4. Separate the tortillas into two stacks of 8 tortillas each. Wrap each stack in paper towels and sprinkle with water. Microwave until warm and pliable, about 30 seconds.

5. Lay out half of the tortillas on the work surface. Spread the bottom half of each tortilla with 3 to 4 tablespoons of the filling, leaving a ½-inch border around the sides. Starting at the bottom, roll up each tortilla and arrange close together in the prepared pan. Repeat with the remaining tortillas and filling. Mist with the cooking spray and drizzle with some olive oil.

6. Bake until golden brown, 15 to 20 minutes.

7. Sprinkle with the scallions and a drizzle of the dip. Transfer to a platter and serve hot, with the remaining dip on the side.

RANCH DRESSING

Makes about 1½ cups

1 cup mayonnaise

½ cup full-fat sour cream or whole-milk Greek yogurt

½ teaspoon dried chives

½ teaspoon dried parsley

½ teaspoon dried dill weed

¼ teaspoon garlic powder

¼ teaspoon onion powder

⅛ teaspoon kosher salt

⅛ teaspoon freshly ground black pepper

Milk (optional), as needed

It's pretty safe to say that everyone loves ranch dressing. A lot of folks use buttermilk to supply the tang, but I have sour cream or yogurt on hand more often, so that's what I call for in my version. Keep it thick when you are using as a dip or thin it down with milk to get the consistency you like for a dressing.

In a medium bowl, whisk together the mayonnaise, yogurt, chives, parsley, dill, garlic powder, onion powder, salt, and pepper. Cover and refrigerate to blend the flavors, about 1 hour. Adjust the consistency with milk to make a thinner dressing, as desired. Serve chilled. (The dressing can be refrigerated for up to 5 days.)

Chicken Parmesan with Vodka Sauce

Vodka Sauce

6 tablespoons (3/4 stick) unsalted butter

1 small yellow onion, finely chopped

4 garlic cloves, finely chopped

2 6-ounce cans tomato paste

1/2 teaspoon crushed red pepper flakes

Kosher salt and freshly ground black pepper

1/2 cup vodka

1 1/2 cups heavy cream

1/2 cup freshly grated Parmigiano-Reggiano cheese

8 fresh basil leaves, coarsely chopped

Chicken

6 boneless, skinless chicken breasts (6 to 8 ounces each)

1 cup all-purpose flour

Kosher salt and freshly ground black pepper

4 large eggs

3/4 cup panko bread crumbs

1/2 cup freshly grated Parmigiano-Reggiano cheese

1/4 cup Italian-seasoned dried bread crumbs

Vegetable or canola oil, for shallow-frying

Assembly

Vegetable oil, for the sheet pan

8 ounces fresh mozzarella cheese, cut into 6 rounds

Freshly grated Parmigiano-Reggiano, for serving

4 fresh basil leaves, for garnish

SERVES 6 With its vibrant sauce, crunchy edges, meaty chicken, and melty, blistered cheese, you simply cannot beat chicken Parmesan. You want to keep the crust nice and crisp, so don't drown the chicken in the sauce. Zippy vodka sauce makes a nice change from the traditional marinara. Just as alcohol is used to make perfumes and extracts, the vodka brings out the flavor of the other ingredients without adding any boozy flavor.

1. **MAKE THE VODKA SAUCE:** Melt the butter in a medium saucepan over medium heat. Add the onion and garlic and cook, stirring occasionally, until the onion is golden, about 4 minutes. Stir in the tomato paste, pepper flakes, 1/2 teaspoon salt, and 1/4 teaspoon black pepper. Cook, stirring occasionally with a wooden spoon, until the tomato paste begins to brown and sticks to the bottom of the saucepan, about 4 minutes.

2. Carefully pour in the vodka (don't let it splash and catch fire!) and stir with a wooden spoon to scrape the paste in the saucepan. Stir in the cream and bring to a simmer. Simmer for 5 minutes to blend the flavors.

3. Stir in the Parmigiano and basil. Season with salt and black pepper. Reduce the heat to very low and keep warm.

4. **PREPARE THE CHICKEN:** Pound the chicken to a 1/2-inch thickness (see Note, page 101).

5. Set up a dredging station in three wide shallow bowls or pie plates: In one bowl, mix the flour, 1/2 teaspoon salt, and 1/2 teaspoon pepper. Whisk the eggs well in a second bowl. In the third, combine the panko, Parmigiano, and bread crumbs.

6. Working with one cutlet at a time, turn the chicken in the flour and shake off the excess. Dip in the eggs, letting excess drip into the bowl. Transfer to the panko mixture and turn to coat, patting to adhere. Transfer to a half-sheet pan or platter.

Continues

7. Place another half-sheet pan lined with paper towels near the stove. Pour ¼ inch oil into a skillet (do not skimp) and heat over medium-high heat until the oil is shimmering. Working in batches to avoid crowding, add the chicken to the oil (the oil should immediately bubble around the edges of the chicken—if it doesn't, heat the oil longer). Fry until the underside of the crust is golden brown, about 2½ minutes. Flip the chicken and cook until the other side is golden brown, about 2½ minutes more. The chicken does not have to be cooked through at this point, as it will be broiled later. Transfer the chicken to the paper towels to drain.

8. **TO ASSEMBLE:** Position the broiler rack a few inches from the heat source and preheat the broiler on high. Lightly oil a half-sheet pan.

9. Spread about 1 cup of the vodka sauce over the half-sheet pan. Add the chicken pieces (they can overlap slightly). Spoon a couple of tablespoons of the remaining sauce in the center of each chicken half. (Leave some of the crisp crust exposed—do not smother the chicken with sauce.) Top each with a mozzarella slice.

10. Broil until the cheese is melted, about 5 minutes.

11. Transfer to a platter, sprinkle with additional Parmigiano, tear the basil leaves over the top, and serve.

Spaghetti Squash and Turkey Bolognese Bake

Cooking spray

1 spaghetti squash (3½ to 4 pounds)

4 tablespoons olive oil, plus more for drizzling

Kosher salt and freshly ground black pepper

10 ounces sliced white or cremini mushrooms

1 yellow onion, chopped

2 carrots, finely chopped

3 garlic cloves, minced

1 pound ground turkey

3 cups Marinara Sauce, homemade (page 126) or store-bought

1 teaspoon crushed Calabrian chiles, or more to taste

2 large eggs, beaten

1½ cups shredded mozzarella cheese

½ cup freshly grated Parmigiano-Reggiano cheese

¼ cup finely chopped fresh parsley

SERVES 6 I love cooking with spaghetti squash. It's an incredibly versatile vegetable that can be used in many ways. I thought that I would have to work hard to convince my squad that they should give spaghetti squash a chance, but it sold itself!

1. Preheat the oven to 400°F. Line a half-sheet pan with parchment paper. Spray a 9 × 13-inch baking dish with cooking spray.

2. Cut the spaghetti squash in half lengthwise and scoop out and discard the seeds. Rub a drizzle of oil on the cut sides of the squash. Season with salt and pepper. Place, cut-side down, on the half-sheet pan. Bake until the squash is tender and can be pierced with the tip of a sharp knife, 35 to 45 minutes. Set the squash aside to cool. Leave the oven on but reduce the oven temperature to 350°F.

3. Meanwhile, heat 2 tablespoons of the oil in a large skillet over medium-high heat. Add the mushrooms and cook, stirring often, until lightly browned, about 8 minutes. Transfer to a plate.

4. Add the remaining 2 tablespoons oil to the skillet and heat. Add the onion, carrots, and garlic and cook, stirring occasionally, until the onion softens, about 3 minutes. Add the ground turkey and cook, stirring occasionally and breaking up the meat with a spoon, until it loses its raw look, about 8 minutes.

5. Stir in the marinara sauce and Calabrian chiles and bring to a simmer. Reduce the heat to low and simmer, stirring often, for 5 minutes to blend the flavors. Remove from the heat.

6. Working over a large bowl, draw a dinner fork crosswise across each squash half to pull the flesh into shreds, letting the shreds fall into the bowl. Discard the skin. Quickly stir in the beaten eggs, followed by the turkey sauce, mozzarella, Parmigiano-Reggiano, and reserved mushrooms.

7. Spread the squash mixture in the baking dish. Bake until the casserole feels firm when pressed, about 45 minutes.

8. Sprinkle with the parsley and serve hot.

Glazed Salmon and Broccoli Sheet Pan Dinner

Apricot-Dijon Glaze

¼ cup apricot preserves

1 tablespoon grainy Dijon mustard

1 tablespoon smooth Dijon mustard (or more grainy mustard)

1 tablespoon soy sauce

1 tablespoon fresh lime juice

2 teaspoons grated peeled fresh ginger, grated on a Microplane

1 garlic clove, minced

Broccoli and Salmon

1 pound broccoli crowns, cut into florets

3 tablespoons extra-virgin olive oil

½ teaspoon kosher salt

¼ teaspoon freshly ground black pepper

4 salmon fillets (6 ounces each), or 1 1½-pound side of salmon

¼ cup finely chopped scallions, white and green parts, for garnish (optional)

SERVES 4 This is one of my go-to recipes when I am short on time. It uses basic ingredients, uses only a single sheet pan, and takes 30 minutes from start to finish! Simple and delicious, it's convenient and quick and has everything that I love. Best of all, it's a flavorful meal that's perfect both for a midweek supper or a fancy company dinner. Serve it with steamed brown rice or mashed sweet potatoes.

1. **MAKE THE APRICOT-DIJON GLAZE:** In a small bowl, whisk together the preserves, grainy mustard, smooth mustard, soy sauce, lime juice, ginger, and garlic.

2. Preheat the oven to 425°F. Line a half-sheet pan with parchment paper.

3. **BAKE THE BROCCOLI AND SALMON:** In a large bowl, toss together the broccoli, oil, salt, and pepper. Spread on the half-sheet pan. Bake for 10 minutes.

4. Remove from the oven. Move the broccoli to the sides of the pan, clearing the center. Place the salmon in the center space and spread the glaze on top. Return to the oven and bake until the salmon is barely opaque when flaked in the center with the tip of a small knife, about 12 minutes. (If you like your salmon more well done, as I do, bake for an additional 5 minutes.)

5. Transfer to plates, sprinkle with the scallions if using, and serve.

Greek Shrimp with Tomatoes and Feta

1/4 cup extra-virgin olive oil

1 yellow onion, chopped

4 garlic cloves, minced

1 28-ounce can diced tomatoes, undrained

1 15-ounce can crushed tomatoes

1/4 cup finely chopped fresh parsley

1 teaspoon dried oregano

1/2 teaspoon smoked paprika

1/2 teaspoon kosher salt

1/4 teaspoon crushed red pepper flakes

1/4 teaspoon freshly ground black pepper

1½ pounds large (21/25 count) shrimp, peeled and deveined

1 cup crumbled feta cheese

1/4 cup chopped fresh dill, for serving

SERVES 6 This is a flavor-filled dish that comes together quickly with an herby tomato sauce with shrimp, topped with feta and roasted until the flavors mingle. Spoon it over rice or mashed potatoes to catch all those delicious juices, or skip the starchy sides and serve with lots of crusty bread. Either way a simple green salad is the best accompaniment. This is one of those rustic dishes that is much easier than it looks.

1. Preheat the oven to 425°F. Heat the oil in a large ovenproof skillet over medium-high heat. Add the onion and garlic and cook, stirring occasionally, until the onion softens, about 3 minutes. Stir in the diced tomatoes (and juices), crushed tomatoes, parsley, oregano, smoked paprika, salt, pepper flakes, and black pepper. Reduce the heat to low and simmer, uncovered, stirring occasionally, until the sauce is slightly reduced, about 10 minutes.

2. Stir in the shrimp and sprinkle the feta on top.

3. Transfer to the oven and bake until the shrimp turns opaque, 12 to 15 minutes.

4. Sprinkle with the dill and serve hot.

Carolina Gold BBQ Pork Chops

5 teaspoons Cajun seasoning

1 tablespoon all-purpose flour

1 teaspoon kosher salt

1/2 teaspoon freshly ground black pepper

4 bone-in pork chops, cut about 1 inch thick

2 tablespoons vegetable oil

Carolina Gold BBQ Sauce

3/4 cup yellow mustard

1/2 cup honey

1/2 cup cider vinegar

1/4 cup packed light brown sugar

2 tablespoons ketchup

2 teaspoons Worcestershire sauce

1 teaspoon garlic powder

1/2 teaspoon kosher salt

1/4 teaspoon cayenne pepper

1 teaspoon sriracha

1 tablespoon canola or vegetable oil

1 small yellow onion, chopped

1/2 cup reduced-sodium chicken stock

Chopped fresh parsley, for garnish

SERVES 4 Carolina Gold barbecue sauce would make a freakin' rubber tire taste good! When it comes to amazing BBQ sauces, there's something about this mustard-based recipe from South Carolina. Its gorgeous golden color makes it stand out from the more familiar sauces that have a ketchup base. In fact, beyond these luscious chops, I also use the golden sauce as dip for chicken wings, nuggets, fries, or grilled shrimp, and as a marinade for grilled chicken or steak. I love to serve the chops alongside potato salad, baked beans, or a tangy slaw. Some rice for the sauce would be good, too.

1. On a plate, mix the Cajun seasoning, flour, salt, and pepper. Dip both sides of the pork in the flour mixture to coat and place on another plate. Let stand for 10 minutes.

2. Heat the oil in a very large skillet over medium-high heat. Add the pork chops and cook, without moving them, until the underside is browned, about 3 minutes. Flip the chops, reduce the heat to low, and cover tightly. Cook just until the chops show a hint of pink when cut at the bone with a small knife, 3 to 4 minutes more. Transfer the chops to a platter and tent with aluminum foil to keep warm. Remove the skillet from the heat.

3. **MAKE THE CAROLINA GOLD BBQ SAUCE:** In a medium bowl, whisk together the mustard, honey, vinegar, brown sugar, ketchup, Worcestershire sauce, garlic powder, salt, cayenne, and sriracha.

4. Return the skillet to medium heat. Add the oil to the skillet along with the onion and cook, stirring occasionally, until the onion is tender, 3 to 4 minutes. Add the broth and scrape up the browned bits in the skillet with a wooden spoon. Increase the heat to high and boil until the broth is reduced by half, about 2 minutes.

5. Whisk in the gold BBQ sauce and bring to a simmer. Reduce the heat to low and simmer until lightly thickened, about 10 minutes.

6. Return the chops and any juices on the platter to the skillet, turn to coat, and simmer just until the pork shows no pink when pierced at the bone, about 2 minutes.

7. Transfer the chops and sauce to the platter, sprinkle with parsley, and serve.

Sheet Pan Jambalaya

Cooking spray

1½ pounds boneless, skinless chicken breasts, cut into 1-inch pieces

1 pound andouille sausage, sliced into ¼-inch-thick rounds

2 green or red bell peppers, chopped

1 yellow onion, chopped

2 celery ribs, chopped

3 garlic cloves, chopped

1 jalapeño, seeded and finely chopped

1½ tablespoons chopped fresh thyme

3 tablespoons olive oil

3 tablespoons plus 1 teaspoon Cajun seasoning

1 teaspoon smoked paprika

1 pound large (21/25 count) shrimp, peeled and deveined

3 cups cooked white rice (from 1 cup uncooked rice)

1 15-ounce can diced tomatoes, undrained

3 tablespoons unsalted butter, melted

Kosher salt and freshly ground black pepper

Juice of 1 lemon

2 scallions, white and pale-green parts only, chopped

SERVES 6 Jambalaya is a staple of Creole cuisine, and although this preparation isn't an authentic version of the Southern classic, this weeknight-friendly, sheet pan rendition will certainly be a welcome addition to your midweek recipe arsenal. And, if you have leftovers, turn them into breakfast. Reheat the jambalaya in a nonstick skillet (adding a touch of water, if needed) over medium-high heat, stirring often, until hot. Reduce the heat to low. Make indentations in the rice with the back of a large spoon (for as many servings as you need) and crack an egg into each well. Cover and cook until the egg whites are set and the yolks are runny, 4 to 5 minutes.

1. Preheat the oven to 425°F. Mist a half-sheet pan with cooking spray.

2. Set the chicken, andouille, bell peppers, onion, celery, garlic, jalapeño, and thyme on the sheet pan. Drizzle with the olive oil, sprinkle with 2 tablespoons of the Cajun seasoning and the smoked paprika, and toss to coat. Spread it out in a single layer.

3. Bake until sizzling, 12 to 15 minutes.

4. Meanwhile, in a small bowl, toss the shrimp and 1 teaspoon of the Cajun seasoning.

5. Remove the pan from the oven. Add the rice, tomatoes (with their juices), and the remaining 1 tablespoon Cajun seasoning to the pan, toss well, and spread out evenly. Arrange the shrimp over the rice mixture and drizzle with the melted butter.

6. Return to the oven and bake until the shrimp are opaque and firm, 7 to 10 minutes. Season with salt and pepper.

7. Squeeze the lemon juice on top, sprinkle with the scallions, and serve.

Pork Tenderloin with Broccolini and Balsamic Butter Sauce

2 pork tenderloins (about 1 pound each), trimmed of silver skin

3 tablespoons extra-virgin olive oil

Kosher salt and freshly ground black pepper

2 bunches broccolini (about 1 pound), ends trimmed

Balsamic Butter Sauce

3 tablespoons cold unsalted butter, cut into tablespoons

2 garlic cloves, finely chopped

1⅓ cups balsamic vinegar

⅓ cup packed light brown sugar

1 tablespoon chopped fresh rosemary

1 tablespoon Dijon mustard

Kosher salt and freshly ground black pepper

SERVES 6 TO 8 Pork tenderloin has a lot going for it: It cooks quickly, is a classy and lean cut, is economical, and is a beautiful canvas for different seasonings. When I am pressed for time, pork tenderloin comes to the rescue, especially this version with broccolini cooked right in the same pan. For a terrific carb accompaniment, go for roasted potato wedges.

1. Preheat the oven to 400°F. Rub the pork with 1 tablespoon of the oil and season with salt and pepper. In a medium bowl, toss the broccolini with the remaining 2 tablespoons oil and season with salt and pepper.

2. Heat a large skillet over high heat until it is very hot. Add the pork and cook, turning occasionally until golden brown, about 4 minutes. Transfer to a half-sheet pan. Set the skillet aside for the sauce.

3. Arrange the broccolini in a single layer around the pork. Roast for 6 minutes. Stir the broccolini and continue roasting until an instant-read thermometer inserted in the thickest part of a tenderloin reads 145°F, 7 to 10 minutes more.

4. Transfer the pork to a carving board and tent with aluminum foil. Turn off the oven and leave the door ajar to keep the broccolini warm.

5. **MEANWHILE, MAKE THE BALSAMIC BUTTER SAUCE:** About 10 minutes before the pork is done, melt 1 tablespoon of the butter in the reserved skillet over medium heat. Add the garlic and cook, stirring occasionally, until the garlic is tender but not browned, about 2 minutes. Add the vinegar, brown sugar, rosemary, and mustard and bring to a boil over high heat, whisking to loosen any browned bits in the skillet. Boil to reduce the liquid by half, about 7 minutes.

6. Remove the skillet from the heat. One tablespoon at a time, whisk in the remaining 2 tablespoons cold butter to lightly thicken the sauce. Season the sauce with salt and pepper.

7. Slice the tenderloin and serve with the broccolini and sauce.

Rigatoni with Creamy Sausage Sauce

2 tablespoons olive oil

1 yellow onion, chopped

4 garlic cloves, finely chopped

1 pound sweet Italian sausage, casings removed

1 cup hearty red wine, such as Shiraz

1 28-ounce can chunky crushed tomatoes (see Note)

5 large fresh basil leaves, torn into bits

½ teaspoon crushed red pepper flakes

1 cup heavy cream

1 fresh thyme sprig, or ½ teaspoon dried

¼ cup finely chopped fresh parsley, plus more for serving

Kosher salt

1 pound rigatoni or ziti

½ cup freshly grated Parmigiano-Reggiano cheese, plus more for serving

1 cup part-skim or whole-milk ricotta cheese, for serving

Note

Crushed tomatoes come in all kinds of textures; some are chunky, and others are more like purees. When you find a brand that has the texture you like (and I like my crushed tomatoes on the coarse side), take note for your next purchase. Or purchase plum tomatoes in tomato juice and use kitchen scissors to snip them into small chunks, right in the can.

SERVES 6 My grandparents emigrated from Italy to America in their twenties. I've often said that my grandmother was the best cook I ever knew. During the summer her garden was bountiful. It fed her family, and the rest of the neighborhood, too. Everything she cooked was homegrown or raised in her yard, and I like to do the same as much as I can, especially during the summer. This easy dish was one she often made especially for my dad. She used ricotta, but my family prefers it with heavy cream; so as a nod to her OG recipe, I still finish the dish off with a dollop of ricotta.

1. Heat the oil in a large saucepan over medium heat. Add the onion and garlic and cook, stirring occasionally, until softened, about 3 minutes. Add the sausage and cook, stirring occasionally and breaking up the sausage with the side of a spoon, until the sausage loses its raw look, about 8 minutes.

2. Stir in the wine, increase the heat to high, and bring to a boil, scraping up the browned bits in the saucepan with a wooden spoon. Cook until reduced by half, about 3 minutes.

3. Stir in the tomatoes, basil, and pepper flakes and bring to a boil. Reduce the heat to medium-low and simmer for 5 minutes.

4. Stir in the cream and thyme, return to a simmer, and cook over medium heat, stirring occasionally, until slightly reduced, about 10 minutes. Stir in the parsley. Remove and discard the thyme sprig.

5. Meanwhile, bring a large pot of salted water to a boil over high heat. Add the rigatoni and cook to not quite al dente according to the package directions.

6. Scoop out and reserve 1 cup of the pasta cooking water. Drain the pasta, add it to the sauce, and simmer to finish cooking the pasta until it is al dente, 1 to 2 minutes. Stir in the Parmigiano and mix in enough of the reserved pasta water to loosen the sauce to the desired consistency.

7. Serve hot in bowls, with a dollop of ricotta and a sprinkle of parsley on each. Pass more Parmigiano at the table for grating.

Angel Hair with Chunky Roasted Tomato Sauce and Burrata

2 pints (about 24 ounces) grape or cherry tomatoes

2 tablespoons extra-virgin olive oil

Kosher salt and freshly ground black pepper

1 pound angel hair pasta

Pinch of crushed red pepper flakes

10 fresh basil leaves, stacked, rolled, and cut into very thin strips

1 8-ounce burrata, drained

Freshly grated Parmigiano-Reggiano cheese, for serving

VARIATION

Smooth Roasted Tomato Sauce: Heat an additional 2 tablespoons extra-virgin olive oil in a medium saucepan over medium heat. Add 2 garlic cloves, slivered, and cook, stirring often, until the garlic softens, about 2 minutes. Add the roasted tomatoes and their juices, 10 whole basil leaves, and the pepper flakes, and bring to a simmer. Cover the saucepan, leaving the lid ajar, reduce the heat to low, and cook, stirring occasionally, to blend the flavors, about 15 minutes. Using an immersion blender, puree the sauce in the saucepan. The sauce will be orange, rather than red, because of the air beaten into it by the blender. (The sauce can be cooled, covered, and refrigerated for up to 2 days, but of course be sure to serve it reheated.) Follow the recipe as directed to cook the pasta, toss with the sauce, and top with the burrata.

SERVES 4 Tomato sauce needs to be simmered for a long time to be good, right? Wrong. This is one of my very favorite ways to make this classic dish, and it is especially good on delicate pasta where its equally delicate flavor can shine. I usually serve the sauce in all its chunky glory, but you can make a smooth sauce if you'd prefer (see the Variation).

1. Preheat the oven to 400°F. Toss the tomatoes and oil on a half-sheet pan. Sprinkle with ½ teaspoon salt and ¼ teaspoon pepper. Roast, stirring occasionally, until the tomatoes are tender and wrinkly and beginning to collapse, about 30 minutes.

2. Bring a large pot of salted water to a boil over high heat. Add the pasta and cook until al dente according to the package directions. Scoop out and reserve ½ cup of the pasta cooking water. Drain the pasta and return to the cooking pot. Add the roasted tomatoes and their juices, the pepper flakes, and basil and toss, adding as much of the reserved pasta water as needed to make a light sauce. Season with salt and pepper. Transfer to a deep serving bowl.

3. Holding the burrata over the pasta, tear open the cheese, letting the creamy filling fall on top. Tear the remaining cheese shell into bite-sized pieces, add to the pasta, and toss to combine. Serve hot. Pass Parmigiano at the table.

One-Pot Orzo with Tomato and Mascarpone

3 tablespoons extra-virgin olive oil

2 shallots, chopped

3 garlic cloves, finely chopped

2½ cups vegetable broth

1 cup canned crushed tomatoes

1 cup heavy cream

1 teaspoon dried oregano

½ teaspoon chopped fresh thyme, or ¼ teaspoon dried

¼ teaspoon crushed red pepper flakes

½ teaspoon kosher salt

½ teaspoon freshly ground black pepper

2 cups orzo

4 ounces mascarpone

⅓ cup freshly grated Parmigiano-Reggiano cheese

8 fresh basil leaves, cut into very thin strips

Basil Grape Tomatoes

2 cups halved grape tomatoes

3 fresh basil leaves, cut into very thin strips

2 tablespoons extra-virgin olive oil

Kosher salt and freshly ground black pepper

SERVES 6 TO 8 This creamy one-pot orzo is made with tomatoes and mascarpone, which makes it such an indulgent and tasty (but low-effort) meal. I could easily eat a bowl of this by itself with a salad or a veg or topped with the grape tomatoes and basil for an extra bit of freshness, but it's also terrific served as a bed for grilled shrimp, scallops, or chicken.

1. Heat the oil in a large skillet over medium heat. Add the shallots and garlic and cook, stirring often, until the shallots soften, about 2 minutes. Add the broth, crushed tomatoes, cream, oregano, thyme, pepper flakes, salt, and black pepper and stir until well combined.

2. Increase the heat to high and bring to a boil. Stir in the orzo and reduce the heat to low. Simmer until the orzo is tender, timing according to the package directions and stirring often to avoid scorching.

3. Remove from the heat. Stir in the mascarpone, Parmigiano, and basil until well combined. The orzo will thicken as it stands.

4. **MAKE THE BASIL GRAPE TOMATOES:** In a medium bowl, stir together the tomatoes, basil, and oil. Season with salt and pepper.

5. Spoon the orzo into bowls, top with a spoonful of the basil tomatoes, and serve.

Pappardelle, Peas, and Prosciutto

1 tablespoon plus 2 teaspoons olive oil

3 ounces thinly sliced prosciutto

½ yellow onion, chopped

1 garlic clove, finely chopped

Kosher salt

1 8.8-ounce package pappardelle

1½ cups frozen peas, thawed

¾ cup heavy cream

¼ cup freshly grated Parmigiano-Reggiano cheese, plus more for serving

Finely grated zest of 1 lemon

Freshly ground black pepper

2 tablespoons finely chopped fresh parsley

SERVES 4 I grew up on a version of this dish. Mom's recipe didn't include meat, but the addition of the crispy prosciutto brings a wonderful intensity to the pasta, and gives it a surprising texture that I love. Not only is this quick and easy, but you also probably have most of the ingredients on hand. When I don't have any prosciutto, I substitute bacon or salami (just brown them in a skillet). Pappardelle is usually sold in smaller packages than other pasta, and while this can be easily doubled for more servings, keep in mind that this wonderful recipe is on the rich side, and is usually enjoyed in smaller portions.

1. Heat 1 teaspoon of the oil in a large nonstick skillet over medium-high heat. In batches, if necessary, add the prosciutto and cook, turning once, until curled and crispy, about 4 minutes. Transfer to paper towels to drain and cool. Crumble the prosciutto.

2. Return the skillet to medium heat. Add 1 tablespoon of the oil, the onion, and garlic and cook, stirring often, until tender, about 4 minutes. Remove from the heat.

3. Bring a large pot of salted water to a boil over high heat. Add the pappardelle and cook until al dente according to the package directions, stirring occasionally. Scoop out and reserve ½ cup of the pasta cooking water. Drain the pasta. Return to the pot. Drizzle and toss with the remaining teaspoon of oil and cover to keep warm.

4. Add the peas and ¼ cup of the reserved pasta water to the onion mixture and bring to a boil over high heat. Reduce the heat to medium and cook until the peas are heated through, about 1 minute. Stir in the cream, Parmigiano, and lemon zest and bring to a boil over high heat. Boil until slightly reduced, about 2 minutes. Season with salt and pepper.

5. Reduce the heat to very low. Add the pappardelle and parsley and toss just to coat—do not overcook. If you like a thinner sauce, mix in as much of the remaining pasta water as you wish.

6. Serve the pasta in bowls, top with the crumbled prosciutto and the parsley. Pass more Parmigiano at the table.

Spaghetti with Spicy Bread Crumbs and Lemon

2 tablespoons plus ½ cup extra-virgin olive oil

1 cup coarse homemade bread crumbs (see Note)

Finely grated zest of 1 lemon

Kosher salt and freshly ground black pepper

1 pound spaghetti

5 large garlic cloves, coarsely chopped

½ teaspoon crushed red pepper flakes, or more to taste

2 tablespoons fresh lemon juice

¼ cup finely chopped fresh parsley

Freshly grated Parmigiano-Reggiano cheese, for serving

Note

Never throw away stale bread. Instead, turn it into bread crumbs. Cut crusty bread (crust and all) into 2-inch chunks. Process in a food processor to make coarse crumbs. (This can take a minute or so.) Transfer to a resealable plastic bag and freeze for up to 6 months. There is no need to thaw the bread crumbs before using.

SERVES 4 TO 6 You'll be hard-pressed to find a pasta recipe that is so simple yet so incredibly delicious. And if you're like me, with an abundance of coarse bread crumbs stored in the freezer in need of a use, this recipe will be a welcome addition. Pasta with bread crumbs is a classic Italian dish that my grandmother always made whenever she had leftover bread. She would also fry up a few anchovies when cooking up the garlic and pepper flakes (the anchovies add wonderful umami flavor and actually melt when you sauté them so you don't see them), but my family prefers this recipe without the little fish.

1. Heat 2 tablespoons of the oil in a large skillet over medium heat. Add the bread crumbs and half of the lemon zest. Cook, stirring often, until the bread crumbs are toasted and golden brown, 2 to 3 minutes. Season with salt and pepper. Transfer the crumbs to a bowl.

2. Bring a large pot of salted water to a boil over high heat. Add the spaghetti and cook until al dente according to the package directions. Scoop out and reserve ½ cup of the pasta cooking water. Drain the pasta. Return the drained pasta to its cooking pot.

3. Meanwhile, heat the remaining ½ cup oil, the garlic, and pepper flakes in a small saucepan over medium heat until the garlic is sizzling but not browned, 1 to 2 minutes. Remove from the heat.

4. Add the garlic oil and lemon juice to the pasta and toss, adding as much of the reserved pasta water as desired to make a light sauce. Mix in the parsley.

5. Transfer to a serving bowl. Sprinkle the bread crumbs and remaining lemon zest on top. Serve hot. Pass Parmigiano at the table.

Spicy Garlic Noodles with Shiitakes

Shiitakes

2 tablespoons vegetable oil

6 ounces shiitake mushrooms, stemmed and torn into bite-sized pieces

3 garlic cloves, minced

1 teaspoon grated fresh ginger, grated on a Microplane

2 tablespoons unsalted butter

¼ teaspoon freshly ground black pepper

Noodles

Kosher salt

6 ounces udon (or other dried wheat noodles, such as spaghetti, fettuccine, or linguine) or soba noodles

1 tablespoon toasted sesame oil

3 garlic cloves, grated on a Microplane

1 tablespoon grated fresh ginger, grated on a Microplane

2 tablespoons hoisin sauce

2 tablespoons sriracha

2 tablespoons fresh lime juice

1 tablespoon reduced-sodium soy sauce

2 scallions, white and pale-green parts only, thinly sliced

2 teaspoons sesame seeds, toasted (see Note)

SERVES 4 These noodles are my idea of the perfect weeknight comfort food. You know . . . those nights when you want something quick, satisfying, and super tasty. These are loaded with garlic and ginger flavor—in fact, I use those two superflavors in both the mushrooms and the sauce. You can keep this vegetarian or amp up the protein by adding a handful of cooked chicken breast, ground pork, shrimp, beef, or tofu to each serving. The Asian noodles cook very quickly, so be sure to have all your prep done before you start cooking.

1. **COOK THE SHIITAKES:** Heat the vegetable oil in a large skillet over high heat. Add the mushrooms and cook, stirring occasionally, until beginning to brown, 4 to 5 minutes. Stir in the garlic and ginger and cook until fragrant, about 2 minutes. Add the butter and pepper and stir until the butter melts, about 30 seconds. Remove from the heat and cover to keep warm.

2. **COOK THE NOODLES:** Bring a large pot of salted water to a boil over high heat. Add the udon and cook until tender according to the package directions. Drain.

3. Heat the sesame oil in the large skillet over high heat. Add the garlic and ginger and stir until fragrant, about 30 seconds. Add the hoisin sauce, sriracha, lime juice, and soy sauce and heat until warmed through, about 1 minute. Reduce the heat to very low.

4. Add the noodles to the skillet with the hoisin mixture and toss to coat. Transfer to bowls and top each with a portion of the warm mushrooms. Sprinkle with the scallions and sesame seeds and serve hot.

Note

To toast sesame seeds, heat a small skillet over medium heat. Add the seeds and cook, stirring often, until the seeds turn from white to golden and smell nutty and toasted, about 2 minutes. Transfer immediately to a plate to stop their cooking.

Gochujang Sesame Noodles with Broccolini

Jammy Eggs (Optional)

4 large eggs

Noodles

Kosher salt

8 ounces udon or other dried wheat noodles, such as spaghetti, fettuccine, or linguine

3 tablespoons gochujang (see Note, page 168)

3 tablespoons reduced-sodium soy sauce

2 tablespoons unseasoned rice vinegar

2 tablespoons light brown sugar

2 tablespoons tahini

2 teaspoons toasted sesame oil

2 tablespoons vegetable or canola oil

2 bunches broccolini, coarsely chopped

4 garlic cloves, minced

3 scallions, white and green parts, thinly sliced

8 fresh basil leaves, cut into thin strips

2 tablespoons sesame seeds

1 lime, cut into wedges

SERVES 4 This noodle recipe is salty, savory, and just a tad-bit spicy, all at once. It is perfect for a busy weeknight, so it is on constant rotation in my house because I seem to always need to get dinner together fast. I like to use udon, but any noodle will do. Broccolini is a good starting point for a vegetable component, but you can use a couple of cups of other veggies, such as broccoli florets, small string beans, thinly sliced zucchini, or carrot rounds. I have included jammy eggs in this recipe because I love their flavor, texture and color. You can also top each portion with rotisserie chicken meat, sautéed shrimp, or grilled firm tofu for added protein.

1. **MAKE THE JAMMY EGGS:** Set up a bowl of ice and water and have near the stove. Fill a small saucepan halfway with water and bring to a boil over high heat. Using a slotted spoon, carefully slip the eggs into the boiling water. Reduce the heat to medium so the water is simmering but the eggs aren't bouncing. Cook for 7½ minutes. Remove from the heat and use the slotted spoon to transfer the eggs to the ice water. Let stand for at least 5 minutes. Gently rap the eggs on a work surface to crack the shells. Working under a thin stream of cold water, peel the eggs.

2. **COOK THE NOODLES:** Bring a large pot of salted water to a boil over high heat. Add the noodles and cook until tender according to the package directions.

3. Meanwhile, in a small bowl, whisk together the gochujang, soy sauce, rice vinegar, brown sugar, tahini, and sesame oil. Set aside.

4. Heat the vegetable oil in a large skillet over medium-high heat. Add the broccolini and garlic and cook, tossing often, until the broccolini stems are almost tender, about 2 minutes. Set the broccolini aside.

5. When the noodles are done, scoop out and reserve about ½ cup of the noodle cooking water. Drain the noodles and rinse well under cold running water until cooled. Stir about 2 tablespoons of the pasta water into the gochujang mixture, reserving the remaining pasta water.

6. Return the skillet with the broccolini to medium heat. Stir in the gochujang mixture and cook until lightly thickened, about 2 minutes. Add the noodles, scallions, basil, and sesame seeds and toss the sauce until warmed through. If the sauce is too thick, add some of the reserved pasta water until you reach the desired consistency.

7. Divide the noodles among four serving bowls and top each with a jammy egg, if using. Serve with the lime wedges.

Vegetables, Big & Small

For generations, vegetables showed up on the dinner table in only two guises: salads or sides. Those were the bad old days. Now, vegetables are often the meal. As a pescatarian for three decades running, I'm thrilled. I love a good veg side dish, and I've become quite attached to the accessibility of high-flavor ingredients that weren't so easy to find a decade ago, preparing vegetables like Gochujang-Roasted Carrots (page 168) and Roasted Delicata Squash with Pomegranate Glaze (page 170). (I remember the first time I cooked butternut squash from *The Fannie Farmer Cookbook*. It literally changed my life. Mom *never* made butternut squash. Maybe it wasn't Italian enough?) But having veg dishes as the star of the table is a new trend that's here to stay. With a little bit of attention to boost flavor, a veggie-forward meal can be as craveworthy and convenient as any meaty meal.

In my family, omnivores share the meal with vegetarians. Serve one of the vegetable entrées with a simply prepared protein (a big grilled flank steak, a roasted side of salmon, some sautéed chicken or shrimp) and give the vegetarians larger portions of the veggie dish. Or you might choose to make two or three of the "smaller dishes" for a vegetarian buffet, accompanied with a crusty, filling bread.

Tuscan Beans with Vegetables

2 tablespoons oil from jarred oil-packed sun-dried tomatoes (or olive oil)

1 small red onion, chopped

3 garlic cloves, finely chopped

1 pint (about 1½ cups) cherry or grape tomatoes, halved

Kosher salt and freshly ground black pepper

1 12-ounce jar marinated artichoke hearts, drained

½ cup chopped oil-packed sun-dried tomatoes, drained

1 tablespoon finely chopped fresh rosemary

6 chopped fresh basil leaves

2 15-ounce cans cannellini (white kidney beans), drained and rinsed

½ cup vegetable broth, chicken broth, or water

½ teaspoon Calabrian chile paste, or ¼ teaspoon crushed red pepper flakes

3 cups packed baby spinach

2 tablespoons fresh lemon juice

Freshly grated Parmigiano-Reggiano cheese, for serving

SERVES 6 TO 8 This saucy skillet of creamy white beans is chock-full of spinach, artichoke hearts, and tomatoes, and brought together with fresh herbs. When I have it for dinner, I am perfectly satisfied, but feel free to grill or roast up some sausages to pump up the protein. Spoon it into big bowls, add a final drizzle of extra-virgin olive oil, and pass some crusty bread on the side.

1. Heat the oil in a large skillet over medium heat. Add the onion and garlic and cook, stirring occasionally, until softened, about 3 minutes. Stir in the cherry tomatoes and season with salt and pepper. Cook, stirring often, until the tomatoes begin to collapse, about 5 minutes.

2. Stir in the artichoke hearts, sun-dried tomatoes, rosemary, and basil. Add the beans, broth, and chile paste. Bring to a simmer. Reduce the heat to low, cover, and simmer until beginning to thicken, about 10 minutes.

3. Uncover and stir in the spinach. Cook, stirring occasionally, until the spinach wilts, about 2 minutes. Stir in the lemon juice. Season with salt and pepper.

4. Serve hot in bowls. Pass Parmigiano cheese at the table.

Sweet Potato and Black Bean Enchiladas

Filling

4 orange-fleshed sweet potatoes (about 2 pounds), scrubbed but unpeeled

1 tablespoon olive oil

½ cup chopped yellow onion

3 garlic cloves, minced

1 to 2 tablespoons chopped seeded jalapeño pepper

2 tablespoons tomato paste

½ teaspoon ground cumin

½ teaspoon smoked paprika

1 15-ounce can black beans, drained and rinsed

2 tablespoons chopped fresh cilantro

Kosher salt and freshly ground black pepper

2 cups grated sharp cheddar cheese

2 4-ounce cans diced mild green chiles, drained

½ cup enchilada sauce, homemade (recipe follows) or store-bought

Enchiladas

Cooking spray

3 cups enchilada sauce, homemade (recipe follows) or store-bought

10 8-inch soft flour tortillas (1 package)

1 cup grated sharp cheddar cheese

Avocado Lime Crema, for serving (recipe follows)

SERVES 4 TO 6 Enchiladas are always winners in my house, and this vegetarian version is a perfect weeknight meal for my squad. They are hearty and filling, and full of flavor without being overly spicy. Smothered in a homemade sauce, they are easy to assemble, feed a crowd, and don't break the bank. You can easily substitute 1 pound chopped cooked chicken, shrimp, or ground beef/turkey for an equal amount of the potatoes to pump up the protein.

1. **MAKE THE FILLING:** Preheat the oven to 400°F. Line a half-sheet pan with parchment paper or aluminum foil.

2. Pierce the sweet potatoes all over with a fork, place on the prepared pan, and bake until fork-tender, about 1 hour. (Or microwave the pierced sweet potatoes for 6 to 8 minutes.) Set the sweet potatoes aside to cool. Leave the oven on but reduce the oven temperature to 350°F.

3. Meanwhile, heat the oil in a medium skillet over medium heat. Add the onion, garlic, and jalapeño and cook, stirring occasionally, until the onion softens, about 3 minutes. Stir in the tomato paste, cumin, and smoked paprika. Stir in the beans and ½ cup water and bring to a simmer. Cook, stirring often, until the beans are heated through, about 5 minutes. Using a large spatula or spoon, mash about one-quarter of the beans in the skillet so they release their starch and thicken the cooking liquid. Stir in the cilantro and season with salt and pepper.

4. Cut the sweet potatoes in half lengthwise, scoop the flesh into a large bowl, and discard the skins (or reserve for another use, such as baked potato skins). Using a fork, coarsely mash the sweet potatoes. Stir in the black beans, cheddar, diced chiles, and enchilada sauce.

5. **ASSEMBLE THE ENCHILADAS:** Lightly coat a 10 × 15-inch baking dish with cooking spray. Spread about 1 cup of the enchilada sauce in the dish. Spoon about ½ cup of the sweet potato mixture in the center of a tortilla, roll to enclose the filling, and place seam-side down in the dish. Repeat with the remaining tortillas and filling. Spread the remaining sauce over the enchiladas. Cover the baking dish tightly with aluminum foil.

6. Bake for 20 minutes. Uncover, sprinkle with the cheddar, and continue baking until the cheese is melted and the sauce is bubbling around the edges, about 20 minutes more.

7. Let the enchiladas rest at room temperature for 5 minutes. Pass with the avocado crema and any optional toppings at the table.

Continues

For Serving

Avocado Lime Crema (recipe follows)

Optional toppings: Shredded iceberg lettuce, Pico de Gallo (page 61), chopped fresh cilantro, chopped seeded jalapeños, sliced black olives, and sour cream

ENCHILADA SAUCE

Makes about 4 cups

¼ cup vegetable oil

¼ cup all-purpose flour

3 tablespoons chili powder

1½ teaspoons dried oregano

1½ teaspoons smoked paprika

1 teaspoon ground cumin

1 teaspoon garlic powder

1 teaspoon onion powder

1 teaspoon light brown sugar

⅛ teaspoon cayenne pepper (optional)

1 28-ounce can crushed tomatoes
Kosher salt

Okay, I admit it: I am not making any claims that this is an authentic enchilada sauce—but I am claiming that it is freakin' fire. The real McCoy is made with dried, soaked, and pureed Mexican chiles for its bulk, but when I learned how to make my own sauce with chili powder and other Mexican seasonings with crushed tomatoes, I never bought the pricey canned stuff again. It comes together easily and I bet you have all the ingredients in your pantry.

Heat the oil in a medium saucepan over medium-low heat. Whisk in the flour to make a roux. Let the roux bubble without browning for 2 minutes. Whisk in the chili powder, oregano, smoked paprika, cumin, garlic powder, onion powder, brown sugar, and cayenne (if using). Add the crushed tomatoes and 1½ cups water and whisk until smooth. Increase the heat to medium and bring to a simmer. Reduce the heat to low and partially cover. Simmer, whisking often, until thickened, about 10 minutes. Season with salt to taste.

AVOCADO LIME CREMA

Makes about 1 cup

1 Hass avocado, coarsely chopped

½ cup Greek low-fat or whole-milk yogurt or sour cream

¼ cup packed fresh cilantro (including thin stems)

2 tablespoons fresh lime juice

1 teaspoon Mexican hot sauce, such as Cholula

1 garlic clove, smashed and peeled

¼ teaspoon ground cumin

½ teaspoon kosher salt

¼ teaspoon freshly ground black pepper

In a food processor, combine the avocado, yogurt, cilantro, lime juice, hot sauce, garlic, cumin, salt, and pepper and process until smooth. Cover and refrigerate until ready to serve, up to 4 hours. It is best used on the day it is made.

Upside-Down Zucchini and Stracciatella Tart

3 tablespoons extra-virgin olive oil, plus more for drizzling

1 tablespoon balsamic vinegar

1 tablespoon honey

¼ cup pine nuts

3 zucchini (about 1 pound total), cut into ¼-inch rounds

Kosher salt and freshly ground black pepper

Half a 17.3-ounce package (1 sheet) frozen puff pastry, thawed

½ cup stracciatella cheese (see Note)

Fresh basil leaves, for garnish

Note

Stracciatella, which means "little rags" in Italian, is the creamy filling inside balls of burrata. You may find containers of stracciatella (sometimes labeled "burrata filling") at specialty grocers and Italian markets. Otherwise, just buy a burrata and cut it in half to scoop out the soft insides, saving the mozzarella shell for another use.

SERVES 6 A savory version of the upside-down apple tarte Tatin, this is fresh zucchini with a puff pastry crust topped with creamy stracciatella cheese. It is one of those dishes that is ridiculously simple to make but looks incredibly impressive. I serve it often for dinner, but it is also an amazing brunch or lunch main course and is especially useful during the summer when you are looking for ways to use up all that zucchini in the garden (like me). And you only need a handful of ingredients! I love it when that happens!

1. Preheat the oven to 400°F. Use a fork to combine the oil, vinegar, and honey in a 9-inch pie plate. Sprinkle the pine nuts in an even layer on top. Shingle the zucchini in concentric circles in the dish and season with salt and pepper.

2. Lightly roll out the puff pastry to remove the crease marks. Place the puff pastry over the pie plate, letting the excess hang over the sides, then fold the excess pastry over at the edge of the pie plate to make a double-thick rim around the border. (Don't worry about the edges that are a little longer than the rest of the dough.) Pierce the pastry all over with a fork.

3. Bake until the pastry is puffed and golden brown, about 25 minutes.

4. Let cool for about 10 minutes. Place a serving plate over the pie plate and invert to unmold the tart. Spread the stracciatella over the center of the tart and garnish with basil leaves. Drizzle with some oil and grind some fresh pepper on top. Slice and serve warm.

Broccoli Rabe with Cannellini Beans and Sun-Dried Tomatoes

Kosher salt

1 bunch (about 1 pound) broccoli rabe, rinsed very well to remove any hiding grit

2 tablespoons olive oil

1/4 cup coarse fresh bread crumbs (see Note, page 152)

3 tablespoons oil from oil-packed sun-dried tomatoes

4 garlic cloves, thinly sliced

1/2 cup slivered oil-packed sun-dried tomatoes, drained

1/3 cup dry white wine

1 15-ounce can cannellini (white kidney beans), drained and rinsed

1 cup reduced-sodium chicken broth or vegetable broth

1/3 cup freshly grated Parmigiano-Reggiano cheese

Kosher salt and freshly ground black pepper

SERVES 6 I'm obsessed with broccoli rabe and love it in every form, but this is my favorite way to enjoy it. This satisfying bean dish is so versatile: Serve it alongside grilled Italian sausages or roasted fish or chicken, or as a vegetarian main dish with a big slab of crusty bread to help drink up the yummy juices. And it can be transformed into a hearty pasta main, too (see the Variation on page 167). However you serve it, the tender and bright broccoli rabe beautifully balances the sweet chewiness of the dark red sun-dried tomatoes and the creaminess of the white beans.

1. Set up a large bowl of ice and water and set near the sink. Bring a large saucepan of salted water to a boil. Add the broccoli rabe to the boiling water and push it down with a wooden spoon to submerge. Cover and return to the boil. Uncover and cook until the broccoli rabe turns a deeper shade of green, about 2 minutes. Drain in a colander. Add to the ice water to stop the broccoli rabe from further cooking. Let stand for 5 minutes.

2. Drain the broccoli rabe well in the colander, discarding any unmelted ice cubes. Pat the broccoli rabe dry with paper or kitchen towels. Cut the broccoli rabe into lengths about 2 inches long.

3. Heat the olive oil in a large skillet over medium heat. Add the bread crumbs and stir to coat. Cook, stirring often, until the crumbs are golden brown, 2 to 3 minutes. Transfer to a bowl. Wipe out the skillet.

4. Heat the oil from the sun-dried tomatoes with the garlic in the skillet over medium heat, stirring occasionally, until the garlic is fragrant but not browned, 1 to 2 minutes. Add the broccoli rabe and sun-dried tomatoes and mix well. Add the wine, increase the heat to medium-high, and cook until reduced slightly, about 1 minute. Stir in the beans and broth and cook until the broth is boiling and the beans are heated through, about 5 minutes.

5. Mix in the Parmigiano. Season with salt and pepper. Transfer to a serving platter or bowl. Sprinkle with the bread crumbs and serve hot.

Continues

Above from left to right: Broccoli Rabe with Canellini Beans and Sun-Dried Tomatoes (page 165),
Gochujang-Roasted Carrots (page 168), Baked Herb and Cheese Mashed Potatoes (page 169)

Rigatoni with Broccoli Rabe and Sausage: Cook 1 pound sweet Italian sausage, casings removed, in a large skillet over medium-high heat, breaking up the sausage with the side of a spoon into bite-sized pieces, until the sausage is beginning to brown, 8 to 10 minutes. Pour off the fat and transfer the sausage to a paper towel to drain. Make the bread crumbs and cook the broccoli rabe and beans as directed in step 4 up to the point of heating the broth and beans through. Meanwhile, cook 1 pound tube-shaped pasta (such as rigatoni or ziti) until al dente according to the package directions. Scoop out and reserve ½ cup of the pasta cooking water and drain the pasta. Return the pasta to its pot, add the broccoli rabe/cannellini mixture (reheated, if necessary), and the sausage. Add the reserved pasta water and the Parmigiano and mix well. Transfer to a serving bowl and sprinkle with the reserved bread crumbs. Serve hot with additional Parmigiano passed on the side. Serves 8.

Gochujang-Roasted Carrots

1 pound carrots

2 tablespoons vegetable oil

2 tablespoons gochujang (see Note)

2 tablespoons fresh lime juice

1 tablespoon reduced-sodium soy sauce

1 teaspoon toasted sesame oil

1 tablespoon pure maple syrup

1 teaspoon finely grated fresh ginger, grated on a Microplane

1 garlic clove, grated on a Microplane

Kosher salt

1 scallion, white and green parts, finely chopped

1 tablespoon sesame seeds, toasted (see page 153)

1 tablespoon finely chopped fresh parsley

SERVES 4 TO 6 These roasted carrots are a delicious side that combines earthy carrots with a sweet and spicy Korean-inspired glaze. These carrots turn out perfectly tender on the inside and beautifully caramelized on the outside and are a terrific accompaniment to just about any meat. I remember when I had to drive miles to an Asian grocer to get gochujang, and now it's available at just about any supermarket. (I also use it in the Gochujang Sesame Noodles with Broccolini [page 154]. Get ready to have a new "secret ingredient" in your cooking.)

1. Preheat the oven to 400°F. Line a half-sheet pan with parchment paper.

2. Cut the carrots into pieces about the size of your index finger. (Cut large carrots lengthwise into halves or even quarters, as needed.) Toss with the vegetable oil on the half-sheet pan.

3. Roast the carrots for 10 minutes. Stir the carrots and continue roasting until beginning to brown on the edges, about 10 minutes. Remove from the oven.

4. Meanwhile, in a small bowl, stir together the gochujang, lime juice, soy sauce, sesame oil, maple syrup, ginger, and garlic.

5. Pour the gochujang mixture over the carrots and toss to coat. Season with salt. Return to the oven and continue roasting until the carrots are tender and glazed, about 10 minutes.

6. **TO SERVE:** Transfer to a platter and sprinkle with the scallion, sesame seeds, and parsley. Serve hot.

Note

Gochujang is a deep red fermented chile paste with a rich, spicy-sweet, umami flavor. A staple of Korean cuisine, it is traditionally added to soups, stews, marinades, and sauces. I also use it to make Gochujang Sesame Noodles (page 166), on grilled cheese sandwiches and avocado toast, dolloped on rice, or as a glaze (which can also be used on chicken, salmon, or pork).

Baked Herb and Cheese Mashed Potatoes

Softened butter, for the baking dish

Kosher salt

4 pounds Yukon Gold potatoes, peeled and cut into 2-inch chunks

2 5.2-ounce packages herb-garlic cheese (such as Boursin), at room temperature, cut into tablespoons

6 tablespoons (3 ounces) unsalted butter, at room temperature

½ cup buttermilk, as needed

½ cup sour cream

3 tablespoons finely chopped fresh chives, plus more for garnish

Freshly ground black pepper

SERVES 8 TO 10 These mashed potatoes with creamy herbed cheese are pure comfort food. But the real beauty here is that the dish can be assembled and refrigerated for up to 2 days. No more last-minute mashing! The cheese adds rich flavor and helps keep the potatoes nice and moist. It is easy and foolproof, and you are guaranteed to get recipe requests every time you serve it.

1. Preheat the oven to 400°F. Lightly butter a 9 × 13-inch baking dish.

2. In a large pot, combine the potatoes with enough cold salted water to cover them by 2 inches. Partially cover and bring to a boil over high heat. Reduce the heat to medium and cook at a low boil until the potatoes are tender, about 20 minutes. Drain well and return the potatoes to the pot.

3. Add the cut-up cheese, 4 tablespoons of the butter, the buttermilk, sour cream, and chives. Mash with a potato masher until the potatoes are combined and smooth, adding more buttermilk as needed. Season with salt and pepper.

4. Spread the mashed potatoes in the dish and dot with the remaining 2 tablespoons butter. Cover with aluminum foil. (The potatoes can be prepared up to 1 day ahead, covered, and refrigerated.)

5. Bake for 30 minutes. Remove the foil and continue baking until the top is beginning to brown, about 10 minutes more.

6. Sprinkle with additional chives and serve hot.

Roasted Delicata Squash with Pomegranate Glaze

3 delicata squash

3 tablespoons date syrup or pure maple syrup

3 tablespoons pomegranate molasses (see Note, page 77)

3 tablespoons extra-virgin olive oil

1 teaspoon kosher salt

1/2 teaspoon freshly ground black pepper

1/2 teaspoon Aleppo pepper (see Note, page 77)

1/4 cup coarsely chopped pistachios

1/2 cup pomegranate arils (seeds)

1/2 cup crumbled feta cheese

2 tablespoons finely chopped fresh parsley

SERVES 6 Delicata squash has my heart. When these babies begin to appear in the grocery store in the fall, I just get so happy. Not only are they cute AF, but they have an earthy, slightly sweet, and velvety flesh that caramelizes beautifully in the oven and a thin, edible skin. The roasted half-moons make a great addition to salads and whole-grain bowls or can certainly stand on their own. This is my favorite way to prepare squash, which will brighten up any dinner table, but especially when it is a holiday meal.

1. Preheat the oven to 425°F. Line a half-sheet pan with parchment paper or aluminum foil.

2. Halve the squash lengthwise, remove the seeds, and cut each half crosswise into half-moons about 1/2 inch thick. Do not remove the edible skin.

3. In a small bowl, mix the date syrup, pomegranate molasses, oil, salt, black pepper, and Aleppo pepper. Place the squash half-moons in a large bowl, drizzle with the syrup mixture, and toss to coat.

4. Spread the squash on the prepared pan. Bake for 20 minutes. Flip the squash and continue baking until the flesh is lightly browned and the squash is tender, 10 to 15 minutes more.

5. Transfer the squash to a platter. Sprinkle with the pistachios, pomegranate arils, feta, and parsley. Serve hot.

Sesame Green Beans with Crispy Tofu

Crispy Tofu

1 14- to 16-ounce block extra-firm tofu

2 tablespoons extra-virgin olive oil

2 tablespoons reduced-sodium soy sauce

1 teaspoon sriracha

2 tablespoons cornstarch

Sesame Green Beans

Kosher salt

1 pound green beans, cut into 2-inch lengths, or haricots verts, left whole

2 tablespoons reduced-sodium soy sauce

2 tablespoons Thai sweet chili sauce

1½ tablespoons sriracha

1 tablespoon toasted sesame oil

2 garlic cloves, finely chopped

1 tablespoon sesame seeds, toasted (see Note, page 153)

SERVES 6 TO 8 Okay, hear me out. Tofu is your friend . . . I know, I know, I know . . . but if I can convince my meat-and-potato-loving husband and kids to eat it and really enjoy it, then maybe you can, too! Tofu is a complete protein, rich in minerals and vitamins, and for vegetarians like me, it's a go-to meat alternative. It has a relatively neutral taste and takes on the flavor of whatever it is cooked with, which is why this dish works so well. The crispy tofu is a wonderful partner to the spicy-sweet green beans. When baking the tofu, the edges will crisp and the insides get warm and pillowy, and I bet you will become a fan, too.

1. **PREPARE THE CRISPY TOFU:** Line a plate with two layers of paper towels and put the tofu on the plate. Top with another two layers of paper towels. Using your palm, firmly press on the top of the tofu to extract excess liquid, taking care to keep the tofu intact. (Or top the tofu with a heavy skillet and let stand for about 30 minutes.)

2. Once the tofu has released much of its liquid, use a large knife to cut the tofu lengthwise into thirds. Flip the 3 slabs over and stack them, then cut lengthwise into 3 columns. Now cut crosswise into fifths, to make 45 tofu cubes.

3. Preheat the oven to 400°F. Line a half-sheet pan with parchment paper.

4. In a small bowl, whisk together the olive oil, soy sauce, and sriracha. Put the tofu in a large bowl, drizzle with the soy sauce mixture, and toss gently to coat, taking care not to break up the tofu. Transfer to a large bowl. Gently toss the tofu with your hands while you sprinkle with the cornstarch to coat. Spread evenly on the prepared pan.

5. Bake for 15 minutes. Flip the tofu over and continue baking until the cubes are crisp and golden, about 15 minutes more.

Continues

6. **MEANWHILE, PREPARE THE GREEN BEANS:** Set up a large bowl of ice and water and have near the sink. Bring a large pot of salted water to a boil over high heat. Add the green beans and cook until just crisp-tender, about 3 minutes. Drain and rinse under cold running water. Transfer to the bowl of iced water and let stand until chilled, 3 to 5 minutes. Drain well and pat dry with paper or kitchen towels and transfer to a serving bowl.

7. In a small bowl, whisk together the soy sauce, sweet chili sauce, and sriracha and set the sauce aside.

8. In a large skillet, combine the sesame oil and garlic and cook over medium heat, stirring often, until the garlic is tender, 1 to 2 minutes. Add the green beans and the sauce and cook, stirring occasionally, until the sauce glazes the green beans, about 3 minutes.

9. Transfer the green beans to a platter. Top with the tofu. Sprinkle with the sesame seeds and serve hot.

Roasted Cauliflower Curry

Roasted Cauliflower

3 tablespoons vegetable or canola oil

1 teaspoon garlic powder

1 teaspoon onion powder

1 teaspoon sweet paprika

½ teaspoon kosher salt

½ teaspoon freshly ground black pepper

1 large head cauliflower, cut into bite-sized florets

Curry Sauce

2 tablespoons vegetable oil

1 yellow onion, diced

2 large carrots, peeled and cut on the bias into ¼-inch-thick slices

1 tablespoon finely chopped peeled fresh ginger

3 garlic cloves, finely chopped

2 tablespoons Madras-style curry powder

1½ teaspoons garam masala

1½ teaspoons ground turmeric

1 teaspoon ground cinnamon

1 teaspoon ground coriander

1 teaspoon ground cumin

1 teaspoon kosher salt

1 14.5-ounce can diced tomatoes, undrained

1 13.5-ounce can full-fat coconut milk

1 15-ounce can garbanzo beans (chickpeas), drained and rinsed

12 grape tomatoes, halved

Finely grated zest and juice of 1 lime

2 cups baby spinach

3 tablespoons finely chopped fresh cilantro

About 6 cups cooked rice (from 2 cups uncooked rice)

Lime wedges, for squeezing

SERVES 6 TO 8 When I was growing up, my mom made cauliflower one way—boiled and tossed with pasta. I never *ever* looked forward to cauliflower night. It was as bland as it looked. Fast-forward to the state of nirvana I felt when I discovered the gloriousness that is roasted cauliflower! Where the heck was this all my life? Roasted in a high-temp oven until charred and crispy at the edges, roasted cauliflower will change anyone's ambivalence about this humble vegetable. I love roasting cauliflower—and my peeps look forward to cauliflower night!

1. **ROAST THE CAULIFLOWER:** Preheat the oven to 425°F.

2. In a large bowl, combine the oil, garlic powder, onion powder, paprika, salt, and pepper. Add the cauliflower and toss to coat. Spread on a half-sheet pan.

3. Roast, stirring occasionally, until the cauliflower is tender and tinged with brown, about 30 minutes. Remove from the oven.

4. **MAKE THE CURRY SAUCE:** Heat the oil in a large saucepan over medium heat. Add the onion and carrots and cook, stirring occasionally, until the onion is tender, about 4 minutes. Stir in the ginger and garlic and cook until fragrant, about 1 minute. Add the curry powder, garam masala, turmeric, cinnamon, coriander, cumin, and salt and stir until aromatic, 15 to 30 seconds.

5. Stir in the tomatoes (with their juices), coconut milk, garbanzos, grape tomatoes, and ½ cup water and bring to a boil. Reduce the heat to medium-low and simmer for 5 minutes to blend the flavors. Add the cauliflower, lime zest, lime juice, spinach, and cilantro and simmer for 2 minutes.

6. Spoon the rice into individual bowls and top with the curry. Serve with lime wedges for squeezing.

Parmesan and Herb Parsnip Fries

Creamy Tahini Dressing

¼ cup tahini

¼ cup extra-virgin olive oil

2 tablespoons fresh lemon juice

2 teaspoons Dijon mustard

2 teaspoons pure maple syrup

1 garlic clove, minced

Kosher salt and freshly ground black pepper

2 tablespoons ice water, as needed

Parsnip Fries

Cooking spray

1½ pounds parsnips, peeled

3 tablespoons extra-virgin olive oil

1 tablespoon finely chopped fresh rosemary

½ teaspoon freshly ground black pepper

¼ teaspoon kosher salt

3 tablespoons freshly grated Parmigiano-Reggiano cheese

1 lemon, halved and grilled (see Note)

Note

Whenever you need lemon halves for squeezing onto food, try to find the time to grill them first. This quick step caramelizes the flesh and lightly sweetens the tart juice. Preheat a ridged grill pan over high heat or heat an outdoor grill on high. Lightly brush the cut sides of the lemon halves with olive oil. Place, cut-sides down, on the pan or grill and cook until the flesh is seared with grill marks, about 1 minute. That's all you need to do.

SERVES 6   I don't know why parsnips don't get the respect they deserve. I think people are indifferent to them because they are unfamiliar with their good qualities, and just write them off as "white carrots." That's really not fair to parsnips. They are earthy like carrots, but parsnips are a bit sweeter, making them a more complex root vegetable than most. Try this dish in which parsnip is the star, and really shines. Once you do, I think you will want to cook with it more often.

1. **MAKE THE CREAMY TAHINI DRESSING:** In a small bowl, whisk together the tahini, oil, lemon juice, mustard, maple syrup, and garlic. Season with salt and pepper. Whisk in the ice water, which will make the sauce creamy. (Cover and refrigerate until ready to serve, up to 1 week. If the sauce thickens, whisk in water to reach the desired consistency.)

2. **MAKE THE PARSNIP FRIES:** Preheat the oven to 425°F. Lightly coat a half-sheet pan with cooking spray and place it in the oven to heat along with the oven.

3. Using a sharp knife, cut the parsnips into "fries" about 3 inches long and ½ inch wide. In a large bowl, whisk together the oil, rosemary, pepper, and salt. Add the parsnips and toss to coat. Spread in a single layer on the heated half-sheet pan.

4. Bake until the fries are tender and golden brown, 20 to 25 minutes. Remove from the oven, sprinkle with the Parmigiano, and return to the oven until the cheese melts, about 2 minutes.

5. Transfer to a platter and serve with the tahini sauce for dipping and the grilled lemon halves for squeezing.

Roasted Eggplant with Chimichurri

Chimichurri

1 cup packed fresh parsley leaves (include the thin stems)

1 cup packed fresh cilantro leaves (include the thin stems)

1 cup extra-virgin olive oil

¼ cup red wine vinegar

2 shallots, chopped

8 garlic cloves, smashed and peeled

1 tablespoon finely chopped red onion

1 teaspoon dried oregano

1 teaspoon freshly ground black pepper

½ teaspoon crushed red pepper flakes

½ teaspoon kosher salt

Roasted Eggplant

2 globe eggplants, cut crosswise into rounds ½ inch thick

Olive oil, for brushing

Kosher salt and freshly ground black pepper

SERVES 6 TO 8 My family loves chimichurri, an Argentine condiment that is tangy, garlicky, and herby all at once. Mixed in a pasta salad, spooned over grilled steak or chicken, tossed with shrimp, or drizzled over eggs, it is always welcome. One of my favorite ways of using it is as a "sauce" for roasted eggplant. Roasting the eggplant softens, browns, and slightly caramelizes it while increasing its flavor, and it beautifully soaks up the zippy chimichurri topping. I have served this as a vegetarian main course along with a salad or a platter of roasted tomatoes with some thick slices of toasted bread.

1. **MAKE THE CHIMICHURRI:** In a blender or food processor, combine the parsley, cilantro, oil, vinegar, shallots, garlic, red onion, oregano, black pepper, pepper flakes, and salt and process until the ingredients are minced and combined. It should be more like a salad dressing than a thick pesto. Transfer to a small bowl. (The chimichurri can be covered and refrigerated for up to 3 days.)

2. **ROAST THE EGGPLANT:** Preheat the oven to 425°F with the racks in the top and bottom thirds of the oven. Line two half-sheet pans with parchment paper.

3. Arrange the eggplant on the prepared half-sheet pans, brush with some olive oil, and season with salt and pepper. Roast until beginning to brown, about 15 minutes. Remove from the oven and flip the eggplants. Return to the oven, switching the positions of the pans from top to bottom for even browning. Continue roasting until they are tender and lightly browned, about 10 minutes more.

4. Transfer the eggplant to a platter. Spoon about ½ cup of the chimichurri on top and serve. Pass the remaining chimichurri at the table.

Spiced Turmeric Couscous

1 tablespoon olive oil

1 cup pearl (Israeli) couscous

1 large shallot, finely chopped

½ teaspoon ground turmeric

2 cups reduced-sodium chicken or vegetable broth

½ teaspoon kosher salt

3-inch cinnamon stick

⅓ cup golden raisins

¼ cup pine nuts, toasted (see Note, page 77)

2 tablespoons finely chopped fresh parsley

SERVES 6 I can't resist perking up plain pearl couscous with some turmeric and cinnamon to make a bright, interesting side. You will love the lively yellow color this brings to a dish. Here, I toast the couscous in a skillet first to bring out its deep nutty, savory flavor. You can also use it as a base for meals in a bowl, such as the Indian-Spiced Turkey Patty Bowls (page 185).

1. Heat the oil in a large skillet over medium heat. Add the couscous and cook, stirring often, until beginning to brown, about 2 minutes. Add the shallot and cook, stirring often, until it softens, about 2 minutes more. Add the turmeric and stir to coat the couscous.

2. Stir in the broth and salt. Add the cinnamon stick, and bring to a simmer. Reduce the heat to low and simmer, uncovered, stirring often to avoid sticking, until the couscous is almost tender, about 6 minutes.

3. Stir in the raisins. Continue cooking until the couscous is tender, 2 to 3 minutes longer. Stir in the pine nuts and parsley. Discard the cinnamon stick and serve hot.

Lemon Herbed Rice

1 tablespoon olive oil

½ cup finely chopped shallots

2 garlic cloves, minced

1 cup long-grain white rice

2 cups reduced-sodium chicken or vegetable broth

Finely grated zest and juice of 1 lemon

1 teaspoon dried oregano

½ teaspoon kosher salt

¼ teaspoon freshly ground black pepper

2 tablespoons finely chopped fresh parsley

2 tablespoons finely chopped fresh dill

SERVES 6 I created this for the Greek Turkey Meatball Bowls with Tomato-Cucumber Salad (page 187), but it is a terrific stand-alone recipe, too. Sometimes plain rice is just the ticket, but often I want a side dish with more "oomph," and this is it. Imagine how good this would be with simply prepared seafood or grilled chicken.

1. Heat the oil in a medium saucepan over medium heat. Add the shallots and garlic and cook, stirring occasionally, until the shallots soften, about 2 minutes. Add the rice and cook, stirring often, until the grains turn opaque, about 2 minutes.

2. Add the broth, lemon zest, lemon juice, oregano, salt, and pepper and bring to a boil. Reduce the heat to low, cover tightly, and cook until the rice is tender and has absorbed the liquid, about 20 minutes.

3. Remove from the heat and let stand for 5 minutes. Fluff with a fork and stir in the parsley and dill. Serve hot.

Bowls
& Salads

When I was growing up, the list of food served

in a bowl was short: cereal, soup, oatmeal, ice cream. Nowadays, I often serve an entire meal in a bowl. A bowl can be a complete, balanced, and simple meal in one vessel. The thing that I love the most about them is they're a unique way to mix flavors and textures while incorporating different food styles. Bowls give us permission to be fearless about assembly, throwing out the rules about foods that go together.

Bowls, hot or cold, are also perfect for entertaining, because the components can usually be made in advance and then it's just a matter of putting it together. Yeah, yeah, yeah . . . We all know that these bowls (salads or not) are full of nutritional qualities that make them good for you, but, damn, they can be so beautiful as well. I am a person who eats with her eyes first.

I also love the idea of a salad as a meal. (I can't imagine Grandma Montelli reading this. The idea of a salad as a meal to her would have been as strange as chocolate sauce on spaghetti.) Now, greens (and their friends) can be the star of the show, and I've offered a selection of main-course salads that are filling and perfectly suited for a meal. I've also included a few side salads because they're a great complement to the sandwiches my family loves. I am very easily bored by a plain salad. Allow yourself to be inspired by the choices at the greenmarket and supermarket and take the opportunity to experiment. You might be surprised at what you come up with. Use the chart on pages 212–213 as your inspiration to mix and match to your heart's content.

Sweet and Spicy Chicken Bowls with Farro and Grilled Pineapple

Sweet and Spicy Chicken

6 boneless, skinless chicken breasts (about 8 ounces each; no need to pound them)

3 tablespoons olive oil

2 tablespoons smoked paprika

2 tablespoons light brown sugar

2 teaspoons garlic powder

2 teaspoons onion powder

1½ teaspoons kosher salt

1 teaspoon freshly ground black pepper

¼ teaspoon cayenne pepper

Farro

1½ cups (about 10½ ounces) pearled farro (see page 184)

1 teaspoon kosher salt

Assembly

6 rings (1-inch-thick) fresh pineapple

Olive oil, for brushing

Pickled Onions (recipe follows) or thinly sliced red onion rings, for serving

SERVES 6 Every weekend, I bake a batch of juicy chicken breasts so they are ready for one of many uses—salads, sandwiches, snacking, or bowls like this one. The breasts come out tender and flavorful and ready for just about anything. I season them with brown sugar and smoky paprika, giving them those sweet and spicy vibes for a combination of flavors that just "work." Here they are put to use with a sweet grilled pineapple and nutty farro.

1. **MAKE THE SWEET AND SPICY CHICKEN:** Preheat the oven to 450°F.

2. Arrange the chicken breasts close together on a half-sheet pan. Drizzle with the oil and turn to coat on both sides.

3. In a small bowl, mix together the smoked paprika, brown sugar, garlic powder, onion powder, salt, black pepper, and cayenne. Sprinkle over the chicken and turn to coat with the spice mixture, being sure to pat the spice mixture that falls into the pan back onto the chicken. The chicken should have a generous coating.

4. Bake for 15 minutes. Flip the chicken and continue baking until the chicken is opaque with a hint of pink when pierced in the thickest part, about 10 minutes more.

5. Remove from the oven and transfer to a plate. Cover tightly with aluminum foil and let stand for 10 minutes.

6. **MEANWHILE, COOK THE FARRO:** In a medium saucepan, combine the farro, 3 cups water, and the salt. Bring to a boil over high heat. Reduce the heat to low, cover tightly, and simmer until tender, about 25 minutes. Drain in a sieve to remove any remaining water, if necessary. Return to the saucepan, cover, and keep warm.

7. **TO ASSEMBLE:** Preheat a gas grill on high or heat a ridged grill pan over high heat. Brush the grates clean. Brush the pineapple rings with some olive oil. Place the pineapple on the grill or pan. Cook the pineapple, with the grill covered and the grill pan uncovered, flipping once, until the pineapple is seared with grill marks on both sides, about 3 minutes.

Continues

8. Transfer the pineapple to a cutting board and let cool. Cut the pineapple rings in half. Cut the chicken breasts across the grain into ½-inch slices.

9. Divide the farro among six wide bowls. Add portions of the chicken and pineapple to each bowl of rice. Top with the onion and serve.

Note

Farro is an Italian variety of wheat berry. Most of the farro sold in the United States is semi-pearled, which means that most of the tough hull has been removed, and the farro will be tender when simmered in water for about 25 minutes. If you have unpearled farro (if not clearly marked on the front label, look on the nutritional label to see if it is identified there), the cooking time will be closer to 45 minutes, and you may have to add more hot water to the saucepan during the longer simmering session. Sometimes it is better to assume it is unpearled and allow longer cooking time, because if it is done sooner, it's a nice surprise. Trader Joe's has a quick-cooking variety that I like a lot—just follow the package directions for instructions and cooking time. If water remains in the saucepan after cooking, just drain the farro in a sieve. One cup of dried farro makes about 3 cups of cooked.

PICKLED ONIONS

Makes 1 pint

1 small yellow onion, thinly sliced

3/4 cup distilled white vinegar

2 tablespoons sugar

2 garlic cloves, slivered

1 teaspoon kosher salt

1 teaspoon black peppercorns

1 bay leaf

You'll be glad you have a jar of these in the fridge when you want a little something to brighten up sandwiches, tacos, salads, or other dishes. So easy to make, but so much flavor.

1. Put the onions in a 1-pint canning jar or covered container.

2. In a small nonreactive saucepan, combine the vinegar, ¾ cup water, the sugar, garlic, salt, peppercorns, and bay leaf. Bring to a boil over high heat, stirring to dissolve the sugar and salt.

3. Pour the hot liquid over the onions and close the lid. Let cool. Refrigerate for 12 hours before using. (The onions can be refrigerated for up to 2 months.)

Indian-Spiced Turkey Patty Bowls

Yogurt Sauce

1 cup low-fat or whole-milk Greek yogurt

2 tablespoons sour cream (or additional yogurt)

1 garlic clove, grated on a Microplane

1 teaspoon ground cumin

¼ teaspoon kosher salt

¼ teaspoon freshly ground black pepper

⅛ teaspoon cayenne pepper

Turkey Patties

2 pounds ground turkey (93% lean)

1 cup panko bread crumbs

½ cup canned full-fat coconut milk

1 tablespoon grated fresh ginger, grated on a Microplane

4 garlic cloves, grated on a Microplane

Finely grated zest of 1 lemon

2 teaspoons ground coriander

2 teaspoons ground cumin

1 teaspoon ground turmeric

½ teaspoon ground cardamom

1 teaspoon kosher salt

1 teaspoon freshly ground black pepper

1 teaspoon cayenne pepper

2 tablespoons vegetable or canola oil

Assembly

Spiced Turmeric Couscous (page 178)

5 ounces baby arugula

1-inch-thick slice watermelon, cut into 12 wedges

¼ cup finely chopped fresh cilantro

SERVES 6 To me, ground turkey is like a blank canvas. It can take on whatever flavor you add to it. Here, I've made it into patties, seasoned with traditional Indian spices and served over neon-yellow turmeric couscous with a layer of peppery arugula, too. A tart yogurt sauce brings it all together and wedges of watermelon cool it down. This dish is definitely not lacking in flavor.

1. MAKE THE YOGURT SAUCE: In a small bowl, whisk together the yogurt, sour cream, garlic, cumin, salt, black pepper, and cayenne. Cover and refrigerate until serving and up to 2 days.

2. MAKE THE TURKEY PATTIES: In a large bowl, mix the ground turkey, panko, coconut milk, ginger, garlic, lemon zest, coriander, cumin, turmeric, cardamom, salt, black pepper, and cayenne until combined. Let stand for 10 minutes.

3. Using your clean, just-rinsed, wet hands, shape the mixture into 12 patties, 3 to 4 inches in diameter. Transfer to a plate or platter.

4. Preheat the oven to 200°F. Line a half-sheet pan with a double layer of paper towels. Heat the oil in a large skillet over medium heat. Working in batches to avoid crowding, add the patties and cook, uncovered, until the underside is golden brown, 3 to 4 minutes. Flip the patties, cover, and cook until the other side is golden brown and the turkey shows no sign of pink when pierced in the center with the tip of a small knife, 3 to 4 minutes. Transfer the first batch to the prepared half-sheet pan and keep warm in the oven while cooking the remaining patties.

5. TO ASSEMBLE: Divide the couscous among six wide bowls, top with equal amounts of the arugula and patties, and add 2 watermelon wedges. Sprinkle with the cilantro. Divide the yogurt sauce among six small ramekins for a dipping sauce. Serve the bowls with the yogurt sauce.

Greek Turkey Meatball Bowls with Tomato-Cucumber Salad

Tomato-Cucumber Salad

1 seedless cucumber, cut into bite-sized pieces

Kosher salt

4 plum tomatoes, seeded and cut into bite-sized pieces

¼ cup finely chopped red onion

3 tablespoons extra-virgin olive oil

2 tablespoons finely chopped fresh parsley

2 tablespoons finely chopped fresh mint

Finely grated zest and juice of 1 lemon

2 garlic cloves, finely chopped

Freshly ground black pepper

Meatballs

Olive oil, for the pan and drizzling

2 pounds ground turkey (93% lean)

1 yellow onion, grated on the large holes of a box grater

1 cup panko bread crumbs

1 large egg, lightly beaten

¼ cup finely chopped fresh parsley

2 tablespoons finely chopped fresh mint

2 garlic cloves, grated on a Microplane

½ teaspoon dried oregano

2 teaspoons kosher salt

½ teaspoon freshly ground black pepper

Assembly

Lemon Herbed Rice (page 179)

Tzatziki (page 63)

4 ounces feta cheese, cut into ½-inch cubes

SERVES 6 We all know that meatballs are great on their own. But they're even better when turned into a Greek-inspired meal-in-a-bowl with herbed rice, veggies, and tzatziki. These meatballs are crispy on the outside and soft and flavorful on the inside. Serve them with pita to turn it into a sandwich if the mood strikes. One timing tip: Salt the cucumber for the salad as your first step in the recipe and move on to prepping other components while it drains. Then finish the salad and let it chill to marry the flavors. When it's time to build the bowl, the salad will be marinated and ready to roll.

1. **MAKE THE SALAD:** Toss the cucumber with 1 teaspoon kosher salt in a colander. I do this in the sink so it can drain. It needs about 30 minutes.

2. Rinse the cucumber under cold running water and pat dry with paper towels. In a medium bowl, combine the cucumbers, tomatoes, red onion, oil, parsley, mint, lemon zest, lemon juice, and garlic. Season with salt and pepper. Cover and refrigerate for at least 30 minutes.

3. **MAKE THE MEATBALLS:** Preheat the oven to 350°F. Lightly oil a half-sheet pan with olive oil.

4. In a large bowl, combine the ground turkey, onion, panko, egg, parsley, mint, garlic, oregano, salt, and pepper and mix with clean, just-rinsed, wet hands. Let stand for 10 minutes.

5. Using clean, wet hands, shape the meat mixture into 24 meatballs and place on the sheet pan. Drizzle with additional olive oil. Bake until the meatballs are browned and cooked through, about 30 minutes.

6. **TO ASSEMBLE:** Divide the rice among four wide bowls. Top with portions of the meatballs and tomato salad. Add a dollop of tzatziki and sprinkle with feta. Serve immediately, with more tzatziki passed on the side.

Firecracker Salmon Rice Bowls

Mango Avocado Salsa

1 mango, cut into ½-inch pieces

1 avocado, cut into ½-inch pieces

½ cup finely chopped fresh cilantro

½ red bell pepper, cut into ½-inch pieces

¼ cup finely chopped red onion

1 jalapeño, seeded and minced

1 garlic clove, minced

¼ cup fresh lime juice

1 tablespoon extra-virgin olive oil

Firecracker Salmon

Olive oil, for the pan and coating the salmon

2 pounds salmon fillets, skinned

2 tablespoons light brown sugar

1 tablespoon chili powder

1 teaspoon ground cumin

1 teaspoon smoked paprika

⅛ teaspoon kosher salt

⅛ teaspoon freshly ground black pepper

Spicy Mayo

1 cup mayonnaise, preferably Kewpie (see Notes)

¼ cup sriracha

2 tablespoons honey

2 tablespoon fresh lime juice

Kosher salt

Assembly

About 6 cups hot or warm cooked white or brown rice

1 seedless cucumber, thinly sliced (see Notes)

Toasted sesame seeds for garnish

SERVES 6 This is hands down one of the best ways to prepare salmon, because it's so darn easy and it is freakin' fire. The rub on the roasted salmon is smoky, sweet, and spicy. (You could use this on almost any seafood, and I also prepare shrimp with it all the time.) The salmon is so terrific, you will easily see how it could be served all by itself as a main course with a veg. But with the fresh mango avocado salsa, crisp cucumbers, and a finishing drizzle of sriracha-infused mayo, this bowl is a masterpiece of flavors, and equally good with either hot or room-temperature rice.

1. **MAKE THE SALSA:** In a medium bowl, mix the mango, avocado, cilantro, bell pepper, red onion, jalapeño, and garlic. Add the lime juice and oil and toss well. Cover and refrigerate until ready to serve. (The salsa is best the day it is made.)

2. **MAKE THE FIRECRACKER SALMON:** Preheat the oven to 400°F. Line a half-sheet pan with aluminum foil. Lightly oil the foil.

3. Place the salmon on the pan, skin-side down, and coat with oil. In a small bowl, mix the brown sugar, chili powder, cumin, smoked paprika, salt, and pepper. Sprinkle evenly over the salmon flesh and pat it on to adhere. Let stand at room temperature for 10 minutes.

4. **MAKE THE MAYO:** In a small bowl, whisk together the mayonnaise, sriracha, honey, and lime juice. Season with the salt. Transfer to a plastic squeeze bottle for piping (or resealable plastic bag and snip off a corner to act as a piping bag).

5. Bake the salmon until the flesh is mostly opaque with a hint of rose in the center when flaked in the thickest part with the tip of a knife, 10 to 12 minutes (or a little longer if you like your fish more well done).

6. **TO ASSEMBLE:** Divide the rice among six wide bowls, spreading the rice into a bed. Top each with portions of the salmon, salsa, and cucumber. Drizzle a zigzag of the mayo from the squeeze bottle. Sprinkle with the sesame seeds and serve.

Notes

- Kewpie mayonnaise is Japanese mayonnaise that is especially creamy and has the tang of rice vinegar. The authentic imported version is available at Asian markets, but you can also find the domestic formula at American supermarkets. If you are sensitive to MSG, know that the Japanese version has it.

- To quick-pickle the cucumbers: Whisk ½ cup unseasoned rice vinegar, 1 tablespoon sugar, 2 teaspoons toasted sesame oil, and 1 teaspoon kosher salt in a small bowl. Stir in the cucumbers, cover, refrigerate for 20 minutes, and drain.

BBQ Tofu Bowls with Charred Corn and Pickled Peaches

BBQ Tofu

1 16-ounce block extra-firm tofu

1½ tablespoons olive oil

1 teaspoon smoked paprika

1 teaspoon ground cumin

1 teaspoon chili powder

1 teaspoon garlic powder

½ teaspoon kosher salt

¼ teaspoon freshly ground black pepper

¼ cup store-bought barbecue sauce

Charred Corn

1½ teaspoons olive or vegetable oil

2½ cups fresh or thawed frozen corn kernels (from about 3 ears)

¼ teaspoon smoked paprika

¼ teaspoon chili powder

¼ teaspoon kosher salt

¼ teaspoon freshly ground black pepper

Assembly

5 ounces mixed baby greens

Pickled Peaches (recipe follows) or 3 fresh peaches, each cut into 6 to 8 wedges

2 Hass avocados, sliced

12 ounces cherry tomatoes, preferably multicolored, halved

1 cup thinly sliced radishes

½ small red onion, finely chopped

Cilantro Lime Crema (recipe follows; optional) or plain low-fat yogurt

SERVES 6 Add this to the list of "Recipes That Made Me Love Tofu." It tastes like a summer barbecue in a bowl, only much lighter, and vegetarian, to boot. The bland tofu gets character with a coating of spices, then a slick of barbecue sauce. (I grab a bottle of store-bought sauce, but if you have some homemade sauce handy, so much the better.) While I like to eat this over mixed baby greens, carb-lovers can put them on a base of rice or rice vermicelli.

1. **MAKE THE BBQ TOFU:** Line a plate with a double layer of paper towels and put the tofu on the plate. Top with another double layer of paper towels. Using your palm, firmly press on the top of the tofu to extract excess liquid. (Or top the tofu with two or three plates and let stand to press and drain for about 30 minutes.)

2. Once the tofu has released much of its liquid, using a large, thin knife, slice the tofu horizontally in half. Keep the two slabs stacked and cut vertically into three columns. Now cut horizontally again into quarters to make 24 tofu cubes.

3. Preheat the oven to 400°F. Line a half-sheet pan with parchment paper.

4. In a small bowl, whisk together the oil, smoked paprika, cumin, chili powder, garlic powder, salt, and pepper. Put the tofu in a large bowl. Drizzle with the oil/spice mixture and toss gently to coat, taking care not to break up the tofu. Spread evenly on the prepared pan.

5. Bake for 15 minutes. Flip the tofu over and continue baking until the cubes are crisp and golden, about 15 minutes more. Remove from the oven, drizzle with the barbecue sauce, and toss carefully to coat, trying not to break up the cubes.

6. **MEANWHILE, MAKE THE CHARRED CORN:** Heat the oil in a large heavy skillet over medium-high heat. Add the corn and cook, undisturbed, until the kernels begin to char on the undersides, 3 to 5 minutes. Sprinkle with the smoked paprika, chili powder, salt, and pepper and stir until fragrant. Remove from the heat.

Continues

7. **TO ASSEMBLE:** Divide the greens among six bowls. Top with portions of the tofu, peaches, avocados, tomatoes, radishes, and onion. I like to make a decorative pattern when I do this. If using, put the crema in a plastic squeeze bottle or a small resealable plastic bag with a corner snipped off. Squeeze a zigzag of the mixture over each bowl and serve.

PICKLED PEACHES

Makes about 4 cups

1 cup cider vinegar

1/2 cup sugar

2 teaspoons kosher salt

1 teaspoon crushed red pepper flakes

1 teaspoon black peppercorns

4 fresh thyme sprigs

3 peaches (about 1½ pounds total), each cut into 6 to 8 wedges

Pickled peaches are a breeze to make. While they are convenient to store in a canning jar, you don't have to pull out the canning pot for a water bath. Just store them in the fridge instead of the kitchen shelf. They will last there for 2 months, but you are going to eat them up in a couple of weeks anyway.

1. In a small nonreactive saucepan, combine the vinegar, 1 cup water, the sugar, salt, pepper flakes, peppercorns, and thyme. Bring to a boil over high heat, stirring to dissolve the sugar. Remove from the heat and steep for 10 minutes.

2. Put the peaches into a 1-quart canning jar or covered container. Add enough of the vinegar mixture to cover. Close the jar and let cool. Use when cooled or refrigerate until ready to serve. (The peaches can be refrigerated for up to 2 months.)

CILANTRO LIME CREMA

Makes about 2 cups

1/2 cup loosely packed fresh cilantro leaves (and thin stems)

1/2 cup sour cream

1/4 cup fresh lime juice

1/2 jalapeño, seeded and coarsely chopped

1 garlic clove, smashed and peeled

2 teaspoons honey

1/4 cup extra-virgin olive oil

Kosher salt

This condiment is an obvious complement to Mexican recipes, but I love how the lime brightens the sweet and savory flavors of barbecue sauce in the BBQ Tofu Bowls with Charred Corn and Pickled Peaches (page 191). I also love this as a salad dressing on sturdy greens like romaine or iceberg lettuce.

In a blender, combine the cilantro, sour cream, lime juice, jalapeño, and honey and process until the cilantro is very finely chopped. With the machine running, gradually add the oil. Season with salt. (The crema can be covered and refrigerated for up to 2 days.)

Ginger Pork Vermicelli Bowls

Cucumber Salad

2 tablespoons fresh lime juice

2 tablespoons reduced-sodium soy sauce

1 tablespoon light brown sugar

1½ teaspoons finely grated fresh ginger, grated on a Microplane

1 teaspoon sriracha

1 seedless cucumber, thinly sliced

Pork Topping

1 tablespoon vegetable or canola oil

2 tablespoons shredded fresh ginger, grated on a Microplane

1 small red Thai chile, seeded and minced

2 garlic cloves, minced

1½ pounds ground pork

2 tablespoons reduced-sodium soy sauce

2 tablespoons fresh lime juice

1 tablespoon Chinese chili garlic sauce

1 tablespoon light brown sugar

Assembly

7 to 8 ounces dried rice vermicelli noodles

2 carrots, cut into thin strips (a mandoline or plastic slicer does the best job)

2 scallions, white and green parts, thinly sliced

½ cup fresh cilantro leaves

½ cup fresh mint leaves

Sesame seeds, for sprinkling

2 limes, cut into wedges

SERVES 4 Ground pork is the star of this bowl, and it is complemented by the sweet and savory flavors from the other bold ingredients in the topping. The rest of the bowl is designed to complement those tastes: the cool cucumber, soft noodles, and crunchy vegetables. Even though there are a lot of components to this bowl, you won't need much more than some simple pantry ingredients and it really does come together in no time; and you can make almost everything well before you start cooking. Consider serving these bowls with tender lettuce leaves to create wraps.

1. **MAKE THE CUCUMBER SALAD:** In a medium bowl, whisk together the lime juice, soy sauce, brown sugar, ginger, and sriracha to dissolve the sugar. Add the cucumber and toss well. Cover and refrigerate at least 30 minutes and up to 8 hours.

2. **MAKE THE PORK TOPPING:** Heat the oil in a large skillet (preferably cast-iron) over high heat. Add the ginger, chile, and garlic and stir until fragrant, about 15 seconds. Add the ground pork and cook, stirring often and breaking up the meat with the spoon, until it begins to brown, 5 to 7 minutes.

3. In a small bowl, stir together the soy sauce, lime juice, chili garlic sauce, and brown sugar until the sugar dissolves. Add to the ground pork mixture, mix well, and reduce the heat to very low to keep the topping warm.

4. **WHEN READY TO ASSEMBLE:** Cook the vermicelli in boiling water according to the package directions. Drain well under warm water.

5. Divide the warm vermicelli among four wide bowls. Using a slotted spoon, add a portion of the cucumber salad. Top with equal portions of the pork topping, carrots, scallions, cilantro, and mint. Sprinkle with the sesame seeds. Serve hot, with the lime wedges.

Cold Vietnamese Noodles with Chicken

Marinated Chicken

2 tablespoons fish sauce

2 tablespoons reduced-sodium soy sauce

2 tablespoons fresh lime juice

2 tablespoons light brown sugar

2 tablespoons vegetable or canola oil

2 garlic cloves, finely chopped

1 pound boneless, skinless chicken thighs

Nuoc Cham

1/3 cup unseasoned rice vinegar

3 tablespoons fish sauce

2 tablespoons fresh lime juice

3 tablespoons granulated sugar

1 tablespoon minced peeled fresh ginger

2 garlic cloves, minced

1 red or green Thai chile, seeded and minced, or 2 teaspoons sriracha

Cold Noodles

7 to 8 ounces dried rice vermicelli noodles (or soba, udon, or linguine)

Toasted sesame oil

SERVES 6 This light and refreshing salad is the perfect summertime meal for entertaining, because you can make all the components in advance and then assemble at the last minute. When I serve it to a group with different eating habits, I put out bowls of chicken (or boneless pork or shrimp) and tofu to please everyone. If you are into outdoor cooking, all of these can be grilled. At a restaurant, you will get a small bowl of the nuoc cham to use as a dipping sauce. But at home, it is easier to put it out in a serving bowl with a small ladle and let the diners add the sauce as a dressing to their portions.

---

1. MARINATE THE CHICKEN: In a small bowl, whisk together the fish sauce, soy sauce, lime juice, brown sugar, vegetable oil, and garlic to dissolve the sugar. Place the chicken in a 1-gallon resealable plastic bag and pour in the marinade. Close the bag and refrigerate for at least 1 and up to 4 hours.

2. MAKE THE NUOC CHAM: In a small nonreactive saucepan, combine the vinegar, 1/4 cup water, the fish sauce, lime juice, granulated sugar, ginger, garlic, and chile. Set over medium-high heat and cook, stirring, until the sugar dissolves; do not boil. Transfer to a serving bowl and let cool. Taste and adjust the seasoning with sugar, vinegar, or fish sauce as desired (it should be a nice balance of sweet, sour, and salty). The nuoc cham can be covered and refrigerated for up to 1 day.

3. MAKE THE COLD NOODLES: Cook the rice noodles in boiling water according to the package directions. Drain and rinse well under cold running water until cooled. Toss the noodles with some sesame oil to keep them from sticking. (The noodles can be refrigerated in a 1-gallon resealable plastic bag for up to 8 hours.)

Continues

Assembly

2 tablespoons vegetable or canola oil

2 cups shredded napa cabbage or green cabbage

2 cups bean sprouts

2 carrots, cut into thin strips about 2 inches long

2 scallions, white and green parts, chopped

1 seedless cucumber, cut into thin strips about 2 inches long

2 cups thinly sliced sugar snap peas

½ cup packed fresh cilantro leaves

¼ cup packed fresh mint leaves

½ cup chopped unsalted roasted peanuts, for serving

2 limes, cut into wedges, for serving

4. **WHEN READY TO ASSEMBLE:** Heat the oil in a large skillet over medium-high heat. Remove the chicken from the marinade, shaking off the excess marinade. Add to the skillet and cook until the underside is browned, about 4 minutes. Flip the chicken over and cook until the other side is browned and the chicken shows no sign of pink when pierced in the thickest part, about 4 minutes more. Transfer to a cutting board and let cool. Cut into bite-sized pieces and transfer to a plate.

5. In a large serving bowl, toss the rice noodles and ¼ cup nuoc cham. Top with the cabbage, bean sprouts, carrots, scallions, cucumber, snap peas, cilantro, and mint. Serve cold, with the remaining nuoc cham on the side as a dressing and bowls of the peanuts and lime wedges for each person to add as they wish.

Thai-Style Chicken and Vegetable Salad

Peanut Dressing

½ cup smooth peanut butter

¼ cup reduced-sodium soy sauce

¼ cup toasted sesame oil

¼ cup unseasoned rice vinegar

Finely grated zest of 1 lime

2 tablespoons fresh lime juice

2 tablespoons sriracha

2 tablespoons honey

2 tablespoons finely chopped fresh ginger

2 garlic cloves, smashed and peeled

Chicken

1½ pounds boneless, skinless chicken breasts

1 teaspoon kosher salt

1 small yellow onion, sliced

3 fresh cilantro sprigs

5 black peppercorns

Salad

1 small head napa cabbage (about 2 pounds), cored and shredded

½ small red cabbage, cored and shredded

2 mangoes, cut into 1-inch chunks

2 carrots, shredded

1 yellow bell pepper, cut into thin strips

½ seedless cucumber, cut into ½-inch cubes

½ small red onion, finely diced

3 scallions, white and green parts, thinly sliced

½ cup finely chopped fresh cilantro

1 cup thawed frozen shelled edamame

1 cup chopped roasted unsalted peanuts, for serving

SERVES 8 TO 12 Thai chopped salad is seriously a party in a bowl. It's chock-full of vibrant, fresh, and crunchy veggies, tender chicken, sweet mango, and the creamiest peanut sauce with a bit of heat from the sriracha. I use poached and shredded chicken breasts here, but you can certainly use rotisserie, grilled, or leftover chicken. To avoid a soggy salad, keep all the parts separate and toss everything together at the last minute.

1. **MAKE THE PEANUT DRESSING:** In a food processor or blender, combine the peanut butter, soy sauce, sesame oil, vinegar, lime zest, lime juice, sriracha, honey, ginger, and garlic and process until smooth. If the dressing is too thick, add a little bit of water to get the desired consistency. Transfer to a covered container and refrigerate until ready to use, up to 2 days. Whisk before serving.

2. **COOK THE CHICKEN:** Place the chicken breasts in a medium saucepan. Add the salt, yellow onion, cilantro, peppercorns, and enough cold water to cover the chicken by 1 inch. Bring to a boil over high heat. Reduce the heat to low and simmer until the chicken shows no sign of pink when pierced in the center with the tip of a small sharp knife, about 20 minutes.

3. Transfer the chicken to a cutting board and let cool. Pull the chicken into shreds. Transfer to a bowl, cover, and refrigerate until chilled, at least 1 hour or up to 2 days.

4. **MAKE THE SALAD:** In a very large serving bowl, combine the napa cabbage, red cabbage, mangoes, carrots, bell pepper, cucumber, red onion, scallions, cilantro, and edamame.

5. **TO SERVE:** Top the salad with the shredded chicken and the peanuts. If desired, add cooked grains. Toss with half of the dressing and serve with the rest on the side.

Grilled Watermelon Salad with Shrimp and Arugula

Balsamic Vinaigrette

½ cup extra-virgin olive oil

½ cup balsamic vinegar

1 shallot, minced

2 tablespoons honey

1 tablespoon Dijon mustard

2 garlic cloves, minced

Kosher salt and freshly ground black pepper

Salad

2 1-inch-thick slices round watermelon

Olive oil, for brushing

1 pound medium shrimp, peeled and deveined

8 ounces baby arugula

Kosher salt and freshly ground black pepper

4 ounces feta cheese, cut into bite-sized cubes

Note

If using wooden skewers, be sure to soak them in water for 30 minutes before grilling.

SERVES 6 TO 8   Combining peppery arugula with sweet and juicy watermelon and salty hunks of feta is a typical summer classic salad. But when you grill that watermelon and add some plump shrimp, it becomes something else altogether. As you've probably guessed by now, what I love about this is all the contrasting flavors and textures. I can't resist nibbling on this before it hits the table, and I bet your fam and friends won't be able to stop eating it once they see it set before them.

1. **MAKE THE BALSAMIC VINAIGRETTE:** In a jar with a tight-fitting lid, combine the oil, balsamic vinegar, shallot, honey, mustard, and garlic and shake until combined. Season with salt and pepper. (The vinaigrette can be refrigerated for up to 1 week. Shake well before using.)

2. **MAKE THE SALAD:** Preheat a gas grill to medium-high. Or build a medium-hot fire in a charcoal grill, letting the coals burn until they are covered with white ash and you can hold your hand right above the cooking grate for about 3 seconds. Brush the grate clean.

3. Brush the watermelon slices on one side only with the oil. Place the watermelon, oiled side down, on the grill and cover with the lid. Cook until seared with grate marks, about 2 minutes. Give each slice a quarter-turn on the grate and cook for 2 minutes more to give the slices a crosshatched appearance. Transfer to a cutting board.

4. Thread about 8 shrimp (held in their "C" shape) onto each of four skewers (see Note) and brush with oil. Brush the grate clean. Grill the shrimp, with the lid closed, for 2 minutes. Flip the shrimp and cook, with the lid closed, until they turn opaque, about 1 minute more. Remove from the grill.

5. In a bowl, toss the arugula with ½ cup of the vinaigrette. Season with salt and pepper. Spread the dressed arugula on a deep platter and sprinkle with the feta. Cut off and discard the watermelon rind, cut the flesh into 1-inch cubes, and scatter over the arugula. Remove the shrimp from the skewers and add to the platter. Serve warm. Pass the remaining vinaigrette on the side.

Holiday Orzo Salad

Kosher salt

1 pound orzo

1 cup sliced almonds

3 ounces baby arugula or mixed greens

1 cup roasted unsalted pumpkin or sunflower seeds

1 cup dried cherries, cranberries, or golden raisins

3 scallions, white and green parts, thinly sliced

1/2 cup chopped fresh parsley

1/4 cup chopped fresh mint

Finely grated zest of 1 orange

1/2 cup Holiday Orange-Balsamic Vinaigrette (recipe follows), or as needed

Freshly ground black pepper

SERVES 8 TO 10 This orzo salad is fresh, bright, festive, and completely irresistible. It can be made ahead of time and is delicious served at room temperature, which makes it perfect on a holiday buffet. There aren't any rules for this dish. Feel free to adapt it to your tastes and to complement whatever else you have going on with the rest of the meal.

1. Bring a large pot of salted water to a boil over high heat. Add the orzo and cook until tender according to the package directions. Drain, rinse well under cold water, and drain again. Transfer to a large bowl.

2. Heat a small skillet over medium-high heat. Add the almonds and cook, stirring occasionally, until toasted, about 3 minutes. Transfer to a plate and let cool.

3. Add the almonds, arugula, pumpkin seeds, cherries, scallions, parsley, mint, and orange zest to the orzo and mix. Stir in the vinaigrette. Season with salt and pepper. (The salad can be covered and refrigerated for up to 6 hours. Before serving, reseason with additional vinaigrette, salt, and pepper.) Serve at room temperature.

HOLIDAY ORANGE-BALSAMIC VINAIGRETTE

Makes about 2 cups

3/4 cup extra-virgin olive oil

1/2 cup balsamic vinegar

Finely grated zest of 1 orange

1/2 cup fresh orange juice

2 tablespoons pure maple syrup

1 tablespoon Dijon mustard

1 garlic clove, minced

1/2 teaspoon kosher salt

1/2 teaspoon freshly ground black pepper

In a jar with a tight-fitting lid, combine the oil, vinegar, orange zest, orange juice, maple syrup, mustard, garlic, salt, and pepper and shake until combined. (The vinaigrette can be refrigerated for up to 1 week. Shake well before using.)

Delicata Squash, Farro, and Arugula Salad

Roasted Delicata Squash with Pomegranate Glaze (page 170), made through step 4

5 ounces baby arugula

2 cups cooked farro or lentils

Pomegranate Dressing (recipe follows)

1/4 cup coarsely chopped pistachios

1/2 cup pomegranate arils (seeds)

1/2 cup crumbled feta cheese

SERVES 8 TO 10 I soon discovered that with a few tweaks and the addition of a sweet-tart pomegranate dressing, my Roasted Delicata Squash with Pomegranate Glaze (page 170) makes a fantastic salad—especially when paired with smoked ham (such as the Raspberry-Chipotle Baked Ham on page 129). If you want to make this into a meal-sized salad with some protein, grilled chicken breast is always a good choice, but of course anything you have on hand, such as shrimp or salmon, will be great.

1. Glaze and roast the squash as directed. When the squash comes out of the oven, transfer to a cutting board. Cut the squash into bite-sized pieces. Let cool completely.

2. In a salad bowl, toss together the squash, arugula, and farro. Add the vinaigrette and toss again. Top with the pistachios, pomegranate arils, and feta. Serve immediately.

POMEGRANATE DRESSING

Makes about 1 cup

1/2 cup pomegranate juice

1/2 cup extra-virgin olive oil

1 tablespoon honey

1 tablespoon Dijon mustard

Finely grated zest and juice of 1 lemon

1/2 teaspoon kosher salt

1/4 teaspoon freshly ground black pepper

In a jar with a tight-fitting lid, combine the pomegranate juice, oil, honey, mustard, lemon zest, lemon juice, salt, and pepper and shake until thickened. (The dressing can be refrigerated for up to 1 week. Shake well before using.)

Tangy Coleslaw

1/3 cup cider vinegar

1/4 cup extra-virgin olive oil

1 tablespoon Dijon mustard

2 teaspoons sugar

1 teaspoon celery seeds

Kosher salt and freshly ground black pepper

1/2 small head green cabbage, cored and shredded

1/2 small head red cabbage, cored and shredded

2 large carrots, shredded

1/2 red onion, cut into thin half-moons

SERVES 8 Every cook needs a go-to recipe for a bright, tangy, not-too-sweet coleslaw to serve alongside sandwiches, barbecued meats, or roasted fish. Here is mine, with both red and green cabbage, carrots, and red onions to provide lots of color and flavor.

1. In a jar with a tight-fitting lid, combine the vinegar, oil, mustard, sugar, celery seeds, 1/2 teaspoon salt, and 1/4 teaspoon pepper and shake until thickened.

2. In a large bowl, combine both cabbages, the carrots, and onion. Add the dressing, toss, and season with salt and pepper. Cover and refrigerate for at least 2 hours and up to 2 days before serving.

Farro, Apple, Pomegranate, and Pistachio Salad

½ cup pistachios

3 cups cooked farro (see Note, page 184)

2 Gala apples, cut into ½-inch cubes

½ cup pomegranate arils (seeds)

¼ cup finely chopped fresh parsley

¼ cup finely chopped fresh mint

½ cup Pomegranate Dressing (page 204), or more as needed

Kosher salt and freshly ground black pepper

Fresh mint leaves, for garnish (optional)

SERVES 6 TO 8 I love all types of grains, but if I had to choose a favorite, it would be farro. It's hearty and slightly sweet with an amazing chewy texture and nutty flavor. It's also high in protein and fiber. I love to make a batch to put into this salad. Filled with apples, pomegranate seeds, pistachios, lots of herbs, and tossed with a sweet and tangy vinaigrette, the final salad is as beautiful to look at as it is delicious to eat.

1. Heat a small skillet over medium-high heat. Add the pistachios and cook, stirring occasionally, until toasted, about 3 minutes. Transfer to a plate and let cool.

2. In a salad bowl, mix the farro, pistachios, apples, pomegranate seeds, parsley, and chopped mint. Stir in the dressing. Season with salt and pepper. (The salad can be covered and refrigerated for up to 4 hours. Before serving, reseason with additional vinaigrette, salt, and pepper.) Garnish with fresh mint leaves, if using, and serve at room temperature.

Warm Lentil Salad with Spinach

Kosher salt

1 cup French green lentils (see Note), rinsed and sorted for stones

5 tablespoons extra-virgin olive oil

1 small red bell pepper, cut into ¼-inch dice

3 shallots, thinly sliced into rings, or ½ cup finely chopped red onion

1 carrot, cut into ¼-inch dice

1 celery rib, cut into ¼-inch dice

5 tablespoons balsamic vinegar

5 ounces baby spinach

Kosher salt and freshly ground black pepper

¼ cup finely chopped fresh parsley

Note

While you can use standard lentils for this salad, French green lentils (also sometimes called *lentilles du Puy*) are smaller and prettier. They are pretty easy to find at the specialty markets these days, but you can also buy them online.

SERVES 4 TO 6 The robust flavors of lentils and roasted salmon pair perfectly, and trust me when I tell you that this salad is so good it can be enjoyed all by itself as a meal. Sometimes, I'll add about a cup of crumbled goat cheese to the salad to round it out. One other tip: I rarely make this the same way twice, taking advantage of the opportunity to use up vegetables in the fridge in place of, or in addition to, the vegetables in the recipe.

1. Bring a medium saucepan of lightly salted water to a boil over high heat. Add the lentils and return to a boil. Reduce the heat to medium and cook at a steady boil until the lentils are tender but not falling apart, about 20 minutes. Drain in a mesh sieve and transfer to a large bowl.

2. Meanwhile, heat 3 tablespoons of the oil in a large saucepan over medium heat. Add the bell pepper, shallots, carrot, and celery and cook, stirring often, until the vegetables are tender, 5 to 7 minutes. Stir in 3 tablespoons of the vinegar and cook until almost completely reduced, about 3 minutes. Remove from the heat.

3. Add the spinach to the lentils, then put the hot vegetables on top to wilt the spinach. Let stand for a minute and mix well.

4. Mix in the remaining 2 tablespoons each of oil and vinegar and season with salt and pepper. Check for seasoning, adding more oil, vinegar, salt, and pepper as needed. (Starchy salads tend to soak up seasonings, so sometimes I find that I need more than I initially think.) Stir in the parsley and serve warm.

Italian Potato Salad

Red Wine Vinaigrette

½ cup extra-virgin olive oil

3 tablespoons red wine vinegar

2 garlic cloves, minced

2 teaspoons Dijon mustard

1 teaspoon dried oregano

½ teaspoon kosher salt

¼ teaspoon coarsely ground black pepper

Potato Salad

3 pounds Yukon Gold potatoes, scrubbed but unpeeled, cut into 1-inch chunks

Kosher salt

8 ounces green beans, preferably haricots verts, cut into 1-inch pieces

3 tablespoons red wine vinegar

Freshly ground black pepper

2 cups halved cherry tomatoes

1 3.8-ounce can sliced ripe olives

½ cup sliced pitted green olives (optional)

½ cup chopped red onion

½ cup finely chopped fresh parsley

3 garlic cloves, minced

½ teaspoon crushed red pepper flakes

SERVES 8 Mom said this salad was one of the first things that her mother-in-law taught her when she was first married, and I'd say that she mastered it. Even now, it's not a picnic or a potluck in our family without this potato salad. (Not to mention her macaroni salad with canned tuna in it.) Yes, it's nostalgic, but it's also a crowd favorite and it's a great changeup from (and less heavy than) the mayonnaise-based version—which also makes it great for a hot day because you won't have to worry about the mayonnaise spoiling.

1. **MAKE THE VINAIGRETTE:** In a jar with a tight-fitting lid, combine the oil, vinegar, garlic, mustard, oregano, salt, and pepper and shake together until thickened.

2. **MAKE THE POTATO SALAD:** Put the potatoes in a large saucepan and add enough cold salted water to cover them by at least 1 inch. Bring to a boil over high heat. Reduce the heat to medium-low and simmer until tender when pierced with a small knife, about 25 minutes.

3. Drain and rinse under cold running water. Let stand until easy to handle. Peel, cut into bite-sized pieces, and transfer to a large bowl.

4. Bring a medium saucepan of salted water to a boil over high heat. Add the green beans and cook them just until they turn bright green, 2 to 3 minutes. Do not overcook. Drain the green beans in a sieve and rinse under cold running water until they are cool. Add to the bowl with the potatoes.

5. Sprinkle the warm potatoes with the vinegar and toss well. Season with 1 teaspoon salt and ½ teaspoon pepper. Add the cherry tomatoes, ripe olives, green olives, red onion, parsley, garlic, and pepper flakes and mix, adding the vinaigrette as you do so. Taste and season with additional salt and pepper, if needed.

6. Serve immediately or cover and refrigerate until cold, about 2 hours. (The salad can be made up to 2 days ahead. Reseason with vinegar, salt, and pepper before serving.)

Your House Salad

This chapter has a lot of "big" salads, but what about the everyday "green salad"?

My mom, bless her heart, served a salad with dinner every single night to her family. It was usually only iceberg lettuce, cucumber, canned black olives, and sometimes chickpeas . . . but nonetheless, we always had a salad. Maybe that's why I've always leaned into salads. I also think putting them together is a creative process and a perfect way to use up odd bits from your fridge.

When it comes to salad, there are no rules. Don't be afraid to think outside the box and play around with what you have. Leftover fajitas? Turn them into taco salad! Extra grilled or roasted veggies? Let's make a Mediterranean salad!

Erase any preconceived salad notions you may have and just have fun—and don't let the salad bore everyone. While I don't want to stifle your creativity, I have a few guidelines:

GET YOUR GREENS ON	THE CRUNCH FACTOR	PROTEINS, COOKED	GRAINS, COOKED
Arugula	Beets	Bacon	Barley
Bok choy	Broccoli	Beans	Brown rice
Cabbage	Carrots	Cheese	Bulgur
Chicory	Celery	Chicken	Farro
Kale	Corn	Eggs	Millet
Lettuce, green or red leaf	Croutons	Falafel	Pasta, whole wheat
Lettuce, iceberg	Cucumbers	Sausage	Quinoa
Mesclun	Nuts	Seafood	Rice, brown
Romaine	Onions	Steak	Rice, white
Spinach	Peppers	Tofu	Rice, wild
Watercress	Radishes		Wheat berries
	Roasted veggies		
	Seeds		
	Tomatoes		
	Tortilla chips		

- Pay attention to the balance of ingredients: Tender and crunchy need to play off each other.

- Be careful of too many starches: You might not want grains, beans, *and* pasta in the same dish. It gets too heavy.

- Use fruit as a sweet accent: Unless you are specifically going for a fruit salad, keep your creation mostly savory and use just a little fruit for unexpected sweetness.

To get you going, I've listed examples of components below. When done right, your salad should be nutritious, seasonal, full of flavor and textures, and of course, beautiful. Honestly, with a colorful palette of so many vegetables and fruits at your disposal, a gorgeous salad is almost a given.

LEGUMES, COOKED	FRUIT	DRESSINGS	MISCELLANEOUS AND UMAMI
Beans (canned)	Apples	Balsamic Vinaigrette (page 201)	Artichoke hearts
Chickpeas (garbanzos)	Avocados	Creamy Tahini Dressing (page 176)	Banana peppers
Edamame	Berries	Green Goddess Dressing (page 230)	Bread (toasted)
Lentils	Dried fruit	Holiday Orange-Balsamic Vinaigrette (page 202)	Capers
Soybeans	Figs	Miso-Carrot Dressing (page 117)	Hearts of palm
	Grapes	Pomegranate Dressing (page 204)	Herbs (fresh)
	Peaches	Ranch Dressing (page 131)	Kimchi
	Pears	Red Wine Vinaigrette (page 211)	Olives
	Oranges (fresh or mandarin)		Pepperoncini
	Pomegranate arils		Peppers (roasted red)
	Watermelon		Pickled veggies
			Sauerkraut

Soups & Sammies

When my brothers and sisters and I were young, we would go outside and play for hours in the snow. When we came inside for lunch, we always knew that we were going to be greeted with a steaming bowl of soup and a melty grilled cheese sandwich. Every. Single. Time. It was Mom's food equivalent of a hug and I'll never forget how that lunch made me feel. To this day, soup and sandwiches elicit the same warm, taken-care-of feelings. The pair is always comforting, and whether you choose to eat them together or on their own, they are both a terrific choice for a meal for so many reasons. They are filling, transportable, mess-free, quick to make . . . and delicious.

And: Nothing fills a house with happier aromas than when a big pot of soup is simmering away on the stove. Whenever I make "Pasta Fazool" (page 218), an entire lifetime of family lunches comes back to me, and I hope my kids get the same sense memory when they make my Vegetable Lentil Chili (page 236) for their families one day. As for sandwiches, we all love the old standbys—I have nothing bad to say about peanut butter and jelly. But I love to surprise my kids with new favorites, like my Chicken BLT with Golden Shallots (page 227) or Blackened Fish Sandwiches with Mango Slaw (page 233). And, move over lunch meat—vegetarian sandwiches are here to stay. I get as many requests for Smashed Bean, Avocado, and Vegetable Sandwiches with Green Goddess Dressing (page 229) as for tuna salad or ham and cheese.

Chicken and Barley Soup with Lemon and Dill

2 pounds boneless, skinless chicken breasts, cut into bite-sized chunks

Kosher salt and freshly ground black pepper

4 tablespoons olive oil

2 tablespoons unsalted butter

1 large yellow onion, chopped

3 carrots, cut into ½-inch lengths

3 celery ribs, cut into ½-inch slices

4 garlic cloves, chopped

1½ cups pearled barley

8 cups canned chicken broth

1 Parmigiano-Reggiano rind (optional), about 6 inches long

3 fresh thyme sprigs

¼ teaspoon crushed red pepper flakes

Finely grated zest and juice of 1 large lemon

¼ cup finely chopped fresh dill, plus more for garnish

2 tablespoons finely chopped fresh parsley, plus more for garnish

Freshly grated Parmigiano-Reggiano cheese, for serving

SERVES 8 TO 10 This soup is light and bright and oh-so-comforting. It's loaded with the perfect balance of tender chunks of chicken, hearty barley, and vegetables in a flavorful broth that is completely awakened by the addition of lemon and dill at the end. There is an old Italian cooking trick that I put to use here—save the rinds from your Parmigiano (it only works with the authentic cheese, not American or others) and add them to soup for an extra layer of flavor and umami. Serve the soup up with some crusty bread and a side salad and you have a cozy meal that will warm you from the inside out.

1. In a bowl, toss the chicken with 1 teaspoon salt and ½ teaspoon pepper. Heat 2 tablespoons of the oil and the butter in a large saucepan over medium-high heat. Add the chicken and cook, stirring occasionally, until the chicken is beginning to brown, about 6 minutes. Using a slotted spoon, transfer the chicken to a plate, leaving the drippings in the saucepan.

2. Add the remaining 2 tablespoons oil to the saucepan and let it heat. Stir in the onion, carrots, celery, and garlic and cook, stirring occasionally, until the vegetables soften, about 5 minutes.

3. Stir in the barley and cook until the barley starts to toast, about 2 minutes. Return the chicken and any juices to the saucepan. Stir in the broth, Parmigiano rind (if using), thyme, and pepper flakes. Bring to a boil. Reduce the heat to low, cover, and simmer, stirring occasionally, until the barley is tender, 20 to 25 minutes.

4. Remove and discard the Parmigiano rind and thyme sprigs. Stir in the lemon zest, lemon juice, dill, and parsley and season with salt and pepper. Ladle into bowls and serve hot. Pass grated Parmigiano at the table. (The soup can be cooled, covered, and refrigerated for 3 days or frozen for up to 3 months. As the soup stands, the barley will soak up the broth. Bring it back to the desired soupiness by stirring in broth or water as needed.)

"Pasta Fazool"

2 tablespoons extra-virgin olive oil, plus more for drizzling

4 ounces pancetta, diced

1 small yellow onion, chopped

6 garlic cloves, finely chopped

1 6-ounce can tomato paste

1 28-ounce can crushed tomatoes

2 tablespoons finely chopped fresh rosemary

1 tablespoon Calabrian chile paste

Kosher salt and freshly ground black pepper

2 15-ounce cans cannellini (white kidney beans), drained and rinsed

2 15-ounce cans garbanzo beans (chickpeas), drained and rinsed

4 cups chicken broth

1 Parmigiano rind (optional), about 6 inches long

2 cups ditalini or other short tubular pasta

5 fresh basil leaves, torn into small pieces

Freshly grated Parmigiano-Reggiano cheese, for serving

SERVES 8 Everyone I know calls pasta e fagioli "pasta fazool," not "pah-stuh a fah-jow-lee," which is how it's supposed to be pronounced. In Italian, *pasta e fagioli* means simply "pasta and beans," and it makes sense that this authentic soup, considered peasant food, is as simple as its name. An herby tomato broth filled with the two star ingredients, it's delicious and warming and reminds me of home. Keep this vegetarian by omitting the pancetta and using vegetable instead of chicken broth. Serving crusty bread with your pasta fazool is a must.

1. Heat the oil in a large saucepan over medium heat. Add the pancetta and cook, stirring often, until it is lightly browned and has rendered most of its fat, about 5 minutes. Add the onion and garlic and cook, stirring often, until softened, about 4 minutes.

2. Stir in the tomato paste and cook, stirring occasionally, until it begins to brown and stick to the bottom of the saucepan, about 3 minutes. Add the crushed tomatoes, rosemary, chile paste, 1 teaspoon salt, and ½ teaspoon pepper, scraping up the tomato paste. Bring to a boil. Reduce the heat to low and simmer, partially covered, stirring occasionally, about 10 minutes.

3. In a medium bowl, stir together the cannellini and garbanzo beans. Measure out half of the mixed beans and set aside in a small bowl. Using a potato masher, mash the remaining beans in the larger bowl into a chunky paste.

4. Stir the mashed beans into the tomato mixture. Add the broth, 2 cups water, and the Parmesan rind, if using, and stir well. Increase the heat to high and bring to a boil. Reduce the heat to medium-low and simmer to blend the flavors, about 10 minutes.

5. Stir in the pasta and reserved whole beans. Increase the heat to high and bring to a boil. Reduce the heat to medium-low, cover tightly, and simmer until the pasta is al dente (it will continue to cook in the soup), about 6 minutes. The pasta will soak up some of the broth, and if it gets too thick, just add hot water to get the consistency you like. That said, it should be pretty thick for all the flavors to blend.

6. Remove the Parmigiano rind, if used. Stir in the basil. Season with salt and pepper. Ladle into bowls and add a drizzle of oil to each. Pass grated Parmigiano at the table. (The soup can be cooled, covered, and refrigerated for up to 3 days or frozen for up to 3 months. It will get thicker as it stands. Bring it back to the desired soupiness by stirring in broth or water as needed.)

Manhattan Clam Chowder

6 bacon slices

1 large yellow onion, chopped

3 celery ribs, cut into ½-inch pieces

1 large carrot, cut into ½-inch pieces

6 garlic cloves, chopped

¼ teaspoon crushed red pepper flakes

1 6-ounce can tomato paste

6 cups bottled clam juice

¼ cup anise-flavored liquor, such as Pernod (not a liqueur, like anisette), or dry white wine

2 large baking potatoes, such as russet or Idaho, peeled and cut into bite-sized pieces

3 fresh parsley sprigs, plus finely chopped parsley for garnish

3 fresh thyme sprigs

1 bay leaf

1 28-ounce can crushed tomatoes

5 6.5-ounce cans chopped clams, drained (see Note)

Kosher salt and freshly ground black pepper

Finely chopped fresh parsley, for serving

Oyster crackers and hot pepper sauce, such as Tabasco, for serving

SERVES 8 TO 10 The three most common clam chowder recipes are "white" New England (with milk or cream), "red" Manhattan (with tomatoes), and clear Rhode Island (the same soup base, without dairy or tomatoes). They share a clean, briny, and slightly sweet flavor thanks to the clams—but that's about all they have in common. This recipe for Manhattan clam chowder has layers of flavor, from the clam broth spiked with anise-flavored Pernod to the tender vegetables that are cooked in bacon fat and the light tomato base that allows the clam flavor to shine. And although he loves all versions, my husband will always choose a bowl of this one first.

---

1. Cook the bacon in a large saucepan over medium heat, turning as needed, until browned and crisp, about 8 minutes. Transfer the bacon to paper towels to drain, leaving the fat in the saucepan.

2. Add the onion, celery, carrot, garlic, and pepper flakes and cook, stirring occasionally, until the onion is tender, 6 to 8 minutes. Stir in the tomato paste and cook, stirring occasionally, until it begins to brown and stick to the bottom of the saucepan, about 3 minutes.

3. Add the clam juice and anise-flavored liquor, scraping up the tomato paste with a wooden spoon. Add the potatoes, parsley, thyme, and bay leaf and bring to a boil over high heat. Reduce the heat to medium-low and simmer until the potatoes are tender, 10 to 15 minutes.

4. Stir in the tomatoes and clams and return to a simmer over medium heat. Cook to blend the flavors, about 5 minutes.

5. Discard the parsley sprigs, thyme sprigs, and bay leaf. Season with salt and pepper. Crumble the bacon and stir it into the soup.

6. Ladle into bowls and serve hot, sprinkling each serving with parsley. Pass oyster crackers and hot sauce at the table.

Note

I use canned clam meat here for convenience, but if you would like to use fresh clams, here's how: First, scrub about 3 dozen littleneck clams well under cold running water. Put them in a large bowl, cover with cold salted water, and let stand for 30 minutes. If not cooking right away, drain off the water, cover with a wet towel, and refrigerate for no longer than 24 hours. Put the clams in a large saucepan with 1/2 cup water. Cover tightly and bring to a boil over high heat. Cook, occasionally shaking the pan, until the clams open. Transfer the clams to a bowl, discarding any clams that do not open, and let them cool until easy to handle. Strain the cooking liquid through a fine-mesh sieve and leave any grit behind in the saucepan. Use the liquid as a substitute for an equal amount of the bottled clam juice. Remove the cooled clam meat from the shells. Coarsely chop the clam meat, if desired.

Shrimp Red Curry Soup

8 to 10 ounces cellophane (clear mung bean) noodles

2 tablespoons toasted sesame oil

4 tablespoons vegetable oil

1 pound large (21/25 count) shrimp, peeled and deveined

Kosher salt and freshly ground black pepper

1 yellow onion, chopped

1 red bell pepper, cut into ½-inch squares

2 tablespoons grated fresh ginger, grated on a Microplane

3 garlic cloves, finely chopped

¼ cup Thai red curry paste

3 cups vegetable broth

1 13.5-ounce can full-fat coconut milk

2 tablespoons fish sauce

1 tablespoon light brown sugar

2 tablespoons fresh lime juice

¼ cup finely chopped fresh cilantro

Sesame seeds, for sprinkling

Lime wedges, for squeezing

SERVES 6 Our oldest daughter, Marcelle, moved to Thailand for a couple of years to teach English. While she was gone, I used to make a lot of Thai food to keep that connection to her. This soup became a family favorite while she was away, and my kids still love it and ask for it all the time. Chicken or tofu is a great substitute for the shrimp, and you can easily sub in cooked basmati rice for the noodles. Best of all, this dish uses just one big saucepan, so you don't have a ton of stuff to wash at the end.

1. Bring a large saucepan of water to a boil over high heat. Remove from the heat, add the noodles, and stir. Let stand until the noodles soften (they should retain some resilience), about 4 minutes. Drain and rinse under cold water. Transfer to a bowl and toss with the sesame oil.

2. Heat 2 tablespoons of the vegetable oil in a large saucepan over medium-high heat. Add the shrimp and cook, stirring occasionally, until they turn opaque, 2 to 3 minutes. Transfer to a plate.

3. Add the remaining 2 tablespoons vegetable oil to the saucepan and heat over medium heat. Add the onion, bell pepper, ginger, and garlic and cook, stirring often, until softened, 3 to 4 minutes. Add the curry paste and cook, stirring occasionally, to sear the paste, about 1 minute.

4. Whisk in the broth, coconut milk, fish sauce, and brown sugar. Bring to a boil. Reduce the heat to medium-low and simmer for 10 minutes to blend the flavors.

5. Stir in the reserved noodles, the cooked shrimp, the lime juice, and cilantro. Cook for about 1 minute, just to heat the noodles and shrimp.

6. Ladle into bowls and sprinkle with the sesame seeds. Serve hot, with the lime wedges for squeezing.

Moroccan-Spiced Vegetable Soup

3 tablespoons extra-virgin olive oil, plus more for serving

1 yellow onion, chopped

3 celery ribs, cut into ¼-inch pieces

2 carrots, cut into ¼-inch pieces

6 garlic cloves, finely chopped

1 teaspoon ground cinnamon

1 teaspoon ground cumin

1 teaspoon sweet paprika

⅛ teaspoon cayenne pepper

4 cups vegetable broth

1 28-ounce can crushed tomatoes

3 15-ounce cans chickpeas (garbanzo beans), drained and rinsed

1 teaspoon kosher salt

½ teaspoon freshly ground black pepper

About 2 cups (about half a 5-ounce bag) baby spinach

SERVES 8 When the humble garbanzo bean takes center stage and gets elevated to the tastiest soup, it's a good thing! Loaded with warming spices and spinach, this dish is even more winning because it's both vegan and gluten-free. You could add a big spoonful of cooked couscous to each bowl for more Moroccan vibes and sustenance.

1. Heat the oil in a soup pot over medium-high heat. Add the onion, celery, carrots, and garlic and cook, stirring occasionally, until the onion is translucent, about 5 minutes. Add the cinnamon, cumin, paprika, and cayenne and cook, stirring often, until fragrant, about 1 minute.

2. Stir in the broth, tomatoes, chickpeas, salt, and pepper. (The beans should be barely covered with liquid; add water if needed.) Bring to a simmer. Reduce the heat to medium-low, partially cover, and simmer, stirring occasionally, until the vegetables are very tender, about 45 minutes. Remove from the heat.

3. Using a potato masher, mash some of the ingredients into the broth. This will lightly thicken the soup as the starch from the garbanzos releases. Stir in the spinach—it will wilt from the heat of the soup.

4. Serve in soup bowls, adding a drizzle of extra-virgin olive oil to each serving.

VARIATION

Moroccan Chickpea and Turkey Soup: For a heartier soup, add 1½ pounds ground turkey (93% lean) to the pot after heating the oil. Cook, stirring often, breaking up the turkey with the side of a spoon, until the turkey loses its raw look, about 8 minutes. You can also substitute ground beef (85% lean) for the ground turkey.

Chicken BLT with Golden Shallots

Chicken

2 boneless, skinless chicken breasts (6 to 8 ounces each; see Note)

½ teaspoon kosher salt

¼ teaspoon sweet paprika

¼ teaspoon dried oregano

¼ teaspoon freshly ground black pepper

6 slices bacon

Gochujang Mayo

¼ cup mayonnaise, preferably Kewpie (see Note, page 189)

1½ tablespoons gochujang (see Note, page 168)

¼ cup chopped Golden Shallots (recipe follows)

1 small garlic clove, minced

½ teaspoon toasted sesame oil

Sandwiches

2 large crusty rolls, such as ciabatta, split open

2 slices sharp cheddar cheese

¼ cup Golden Shallots (recipe follows)

4 slices tomato

2 Boston lettuce leaves

MAKES 2 SANDWICHES The last time I made these sandwiches, my son John Paul said that he dreamt about it for a week. He's not one to exaggerate, so I believe it. Chicken that's juicy and tender with extra flavor from bacon fat, melty cheddar, spicy mayo, golden shallots, crisp bacon strips, fresh tomato, and tender lettuce all sandwiched between crusty bread. This delicious play on a classic BLT is hearty, filled with BIG flavors . . . and yes, the stuff that dreams are made of.

1. **PREPARE THE CHICKEN:** Working with one at a time, put a chicken breast between two sheets of plastic wrap (or slip into a 1-gallon resealable storage bag) and pound with a flat meat pounder or rolling pin until ½ inch thick. In a small bowl, mix the salt, paprika, oregano, and pepper in a small bowl and sprinkle on both sides of the chicken.

2. Cook the bacon in a large skillet over medium heat, turning occasionally, until crisp and browned, about 8 minutes. Transfer the bacon to paper towels to drain. Leave the bacon fat in the skillet.

3. Add the chicken to the bacon fat and cook until golden brown on the underside, about 4 minutes. Flip the chicken over and cook until the chicken shows no sign of pink when cut in the thickest part with a small, sharp knife, about 4 minutes more. Transfer the chicken to a carving board.

4. **MAKE THE GOCHUJANG MAYONNAISE:** Mix the mayonnaise, gochujang, shallots, garlic, and sesame oil in a small bowl.

5. **ASSEMBLE THE SANDWICHES:** Preheat the broiler to high. Set the rolls cut-side up on a broiler pan and toast the rolls but be careful not to burn them.

Continues

Note

If your chicken breasts are especially large, such as a single one that is 10 to 12 ounces, cut it in half through the middle vertically to get 2 portions. When pounded, they will be the right size. The individually packed chicken breast halves at warehouse clubs are usually smaller, about 6 ounces each.

6. For each sandwich, spread a toasted roll with the mayonnaise (refrigerate remaining mayonnaise for up to 3 days). Add a chicken breast to the bottom of the roll and cover with a cheddar slice. Return to the broiler and broil until the cheese melts, about 1 minute.

7. Top each with 3 bacon slices, broken to fit, some shallots, 2 tomato slices, and a lettuce leaf. Cap each with a roll top, cut in half, and serve.

GOLDEN SHALLOTS

Makes about ½ cup

3 tablespoons olive oil

4 or 5 large shallots, cut into thin rings

Kosher salt and freshly ground black pepper

In addition to using these on sandwiches, I like adding them to a vinaigrette.

1. Heat the olive oil in a medium skillet over medium heat. Add the shallots and cook, stirring occasionally, until softened, about 4 minutes.

2. Reduce the heat to medium-low and cook, stirring often, until the shallots are golden and tender, about 4 minutes more. Season with salt and pepper. Using a slotted spoon, transfer the shallots to paper towels to drain. (The shallots can be covered and refrigerated for up to 1 week.)

Smashed Bean, Avocado, and Vegetable Sandwiches with Green Goddess Dressing

Bean Smash

1 15-ounce can cannellini (white kidney beans), drained and rinsed

2 tablespoons finely chopped fresh parsley

Finely grated zest and juice of ½ lemon

1 tablespoon extra-virgin olive oil

1 garlic clove, minced

Kosher salt and freshly ground black pepper

Avocado Smash

2 Hass avocados, halved and pitted

Kosher salt and freshly ground black pepper

Sandwiches

8 slices crusty Italian bread, toasted

8 slices heirloom tomatoes

½ seedless cucumber, cut into ribbons (see Note)

1 cup pea shoots

Pickled Onions (page 184)

Kosher salt and freshly ground black pepper

About ½ cup Green Goddess Dressing (recipe follows)

MAKES 4 SANDWICHES This combination makes a perfect veggie sandwich, but you will come up with your own creations to go with the bean and avocado spreads. For example, try baby spinach or lettuce instead of the pea shoots, or shredded carrots for the cucumbers. It's all about playing with the crunch of the bread and the smoothness of the mash. To make it vegan, skip the dressing or use a plant-based yogurt.

1. **MAKE THE BEAN SMASH:** In a medium bowl, combine the beans, parsley, lemon zest, lemon juice, oil, and garlic and mash with a potato masher or large fork until spreadable. Season with salt and pepper.

2. **MAKE THE AVOCADO SMASH:** Scoop the avocado flesh into a medium bowl and mash with a large fork until spreadable. Season with salt and pepper.

3. **ASSEMBLE THE SANDWICHES:** Spread 4 of the toasted bread slices with equal amounts of the white bean smash and the other 4 toasted bread slices with the avocado smash. For each sandwich, top the avocado-spread slices with 2 tomato slices, a few cucumber ribbons, a sprinkle of pea shoots, and a few pickled onions. Season with salt and pepper. Drizzle with about 2 tablespoons of the Green Goddess dressing. Top with the bean-spread slices, spread-side down. Cut in half and serve.

Note

Cucumber ribbons look cool and are easy to prepare. Seedless (sometimes called English) cucumbers are firmer and less watery than standard cukes and make the best ribbons. Cut the cucumber in half crosswise. Using a swivel vegetable peeler, press hard on the cucumber as you draw the peeler from top to bottom to shave ribbons from the vegetable. The harder you press, the thicker the ribbon. Pat the ribbons dry with paper towels.

Continues

GREEN GODDESS DRESSING

Makes about 1 cup

½ cup whole-milk Greek yogurt

½ cup packed assorted fresh herbs, such as dill, mint, basil, oregano, and cilantro

½ cup packed fresh parsley leaves

1 scallion, white and green parts, chopped

1 tablespoon finely chopped fresh chives

1 tablespoon extra-virgin olive oil

1 tablespoon dill pickle or caper brine

1 garlic clove, minced

1½ teaspoons drained capers

½ teaspoon kosher salt

¼ teaspoon freshly ground black pepper

Green Goddess dressing has become a salad classic, with a beautiful verdant color provided by plenty of herbs. It is also a great sandwich spread and dip. The original recipe, now over a hundred years old, featured tarragon, scallions, and anchovies, but I prefer to mix it up and make it more of a showcase for using leftover herbs of any kind and skip the anchovies. Yogurt makes it lighter than the old-school mayo version.

In a food processor, combine the yogurt, herbs, parsley, scallion, chives, oil, brine, garlic, capers, salt, and pepper and process until the dressing is smooth and combined. Transfer to a bowl, cover, and refrigerate until serving. (The dressing can be refrigerated for up to 3 days.)

Blackened Fish Sandwiches with Mango Slaw

Cilantro Mayo

3 tablespoons mayonnaise

3 tablespoons Greek low-fat yogurt

2 tablespoons chopped fresh cilantro

2 teaspoons fresh lime juice

Mango Slaw

2 tablespoons fresh lime juice

1 teaspoon honey

1 8-ounce bag coleslaw mix (about 2½ cups)

1 cup ½-inch chunks mango

Kosher salt and freshly ground black pepper

⅓ cup Cajun seasoning

1 stick (4 ounces) unsalted butter, melted

4 skinless fish fillets (6 ounces each), such as cod, flounder, tilapia, grouper, or mahimahi

2 tablespoons vegetable oil

4 kaiser or ciabatta rolls, split, buttered, and toasted

MAKES 4 SANDWICHES If you were to ask my son Patrick about his favorite recipe of mine, his answer will always be this sandwich. I've made it for years now and when he was in college and used to come home to visit this was always the first thing he requested. And since food is love, of course I was always more than happy to oblige.

1. **MAKE THE CILANTRO MAYO:** In a small bowl, stir together the mayonnaise, yogurt, cilantro, and lime juice.

2. **MAKE THE MANGO SLAW:** In a medium bowl, whisk together the lime juice and honey. Add the coleslaw and mango and toss to combine. Season with salt and pepper.

3. On a dinner plate, mix the Cajun seasoning and 1 teaspoon kosher salt. Pour the melted butter into a shallow dish or pie plate. Dip the fish in the butter to coat on both sides. Transfer to the plate with the spices and turn to coat. Place on another plate.

4. Heat a large cast-iron skillet over medium-high heat. Add the oil and heat until shimmering. Working in batches if necessary to avoid crowding, add the fish and cook, turning once, until the fish flakes easily with the tip of a knife, about 5 minutes, depending on the thickness of the fillet. (I always turn on my overhead fan and open the window when I do this. The frying creates quite a bit of smoke.)

5. For each sandwich, spread a few tablespoons of the mayonnaise over a toasted bun. (Refrigerate the remaining mayonnaise for up to 3 days.) Place a fish fillet on the bottom half of the roll. Add a spoonful of slaw. Cap with the roll top and serve with the remaining slaw on the side.

Grilled Steak Gyros with Tzatziki and Tomato-Feta Salsa

Marinated Flank Steak

⅓ cup extra-virgin olive oil

2 tablespoons fresh lemon juice

2 teaspoons dried oregano

2 garlic cloves, minced

1 teaspoon kosher salt

¼ teaspoon freshly ground black pepper

1 flank steak (about 1½ pounds)

Tomato-Feta Salsa

1 cucumber, peeled, seeded, and cut into ½-inch pieces

2 small Roma tomatoes, seeded and cut into ½-inch pieces

½ cup crumbled feta cheese

3 tablespoons finely chopped red onion

1 small jalapeño, seeded and minced

2 tablespoons finely chopped fresh parsley

2 tablespoons finely chopped fresh mint

2 tablespoons fresh lime juice

Kosher salt and freshly ground black pepper

Gyros

6 flatbreads or no-pocket pita breads

Tzatziki (page 63)

6 large red or green lettuce leaves

MAKES 6 GYROS I love to marinate and grill flank steak—and then slice it nice and thin—for this take on a Greek favorite. To give it a real gyro feel, I serve it on flatbread with lettuce, tomato-feta salsa, and an incredibly flavorful tzatziki sauce. Set everything out and let everyone stuff their pitas with whatever they'd like.

1. **MARINATE THE FLANK STEAK:** Mix the oil, lemon juice, oregano, garlic, salt, and pepper in a 1-gallon resealable plastic bag. Add the steak, press out the air, and seal the bag. Refrigerate, turning the bag occasionally, to marinate for at least 1 hour and up to 4 hours.

2. **MAKE THE TOMATO-FETA SALSA:** In a medium bowl, mix the cucumber, tomatoes, feta, onion, jalapeño, parsley, mint, and lime juice. Season with salt and pepper. Cover and refrigerate until ready to serve.

3. Preheat a gas grill on high heat or heat a cast-iron skillet over high heat. Remove the steak from the bag and shake off the excess marinade. Grill with the lid closed (or place in the skillet) until the underside is browned, about 4 minutes. Turn and grill with the lid closed (or cook) until the other side is browned, 3 to 4 minutes more, for medium-rare meat. Transfer to a carving board and let stand for 5 to 10 minutes.

4. **FOR THE GYROS:** If you have the grill going, add the flatbreads to the grill and toast until heated through, about 30 seconds per side. Otherwise, preheat the oven to 400°F. Place the flatbreads directly on the oven racks and bake until heated through, about 5 minutes.

5. Using a thin sharp knife, cut the steak across the grain into thin slices. Transfer the sliced steak to a platter and pour any carving juices on top.

6. To serve, place the sliced steak, tzatziki, lettuce leaves, salsa, and warm flatbread on the table. Let each person stack a flatbread with a lettuce leaf, sliced steak, a spoonful of tzatziki, and a spoonful of the salsa, and roll to eat.

Vegetable Lentil Chili

3 tablespoons olive oil

1 yellow onion, chopped

4 garlic cloves, chopped

2 carrots, peeled and cut into ½-inch pieces

2 celery ribs, cut into ½-inch pieces

1 medium zucchini, cut into ½-inch pieces

1 red bell pepper, cut into ½-inch pieces

1 jalapeño, seeded and finely chopped

2 tablespoons chili powder

1 tablespoon ground cumin

2 teaspoons smoked paprika

1 teaspoon kosher salt

½ teaspoon freshly ground black pepper

½ teaspoon crushed red pepper flakes

¼ cup tomato paste

1 28-ounce can crushed tomatoes

2 cups dried lentils, rinsed and picked over for stones

2 cups vegetable broth

1 canned chipotle pepper in adobo sauce, finely chopped

2 15- to 19-ounce cans kidney or black beans, drained and rinsed

¼ cup finely chopped fresh cilantro

Toppings of choice (see Note)

SERVES 8 TO 10 Lentils provide a satisfying alternative to meat in this vegetarian chili. The warm spices bring rich, comforting, hearty, and delicious flavors. You'll never miss the meat! But trust me, you don't have to be a meat-free eater to enjoy this. I have a house full of carnivores who love this version just as much as traditional chili. I like to serve it over rice with a side of cornbread and lots of toppings (see Note) and let everyone dig in.

1. Heat the oil in a large heavy saucepan over medium heat. Add the onion and garlic and cook, stirring occasionally, until softened, about 3 minutes. Add the carrots, celery, zucchini, bell pepper, and jalapeño and cook, stirring occasionally, until softened, about 4 minutes.

2. Add the chili powder, cumin, paprika, salt, black pepper, and pepper flakes and stir until fragrant, about 30 seconds. Stir in the tomato paste and cook, stirring occasionally, until it begins to brown and stick to the bottom of the pot, 3 to 4 minutes. Add the tomatoes and stir to scrape up the tomato paste.

3. Add the lentils, broth, and chipotle and stir well. Bring to a boil over high heat. Reduce the heat to medium-low and simmer, stirring occasionally, until the lentils are tender, about 40 minutes. If the chili seems too thick, stir in water as needed.

4. Stir in the beans and simmer until the chili thickens and the beans are hot, 10 to 15 minutes. Stir in the cilantro.

5. Spoon the chili into soup bowls and serve with your choice of toppings. (The chili can be cooled, covered, and refrigerated for up to 5 days or frozen up to 3 months. The chili will thicken upon standing. When reheating, add water to reach the desired consistency.)

Note

Put out bowls of any of the following (you know the drill): chopped avocados, onions, scallions, fresh jalapeños, crumbled tortilla chips, and/or sour cream.

Sloppy Joe Hand Pies

Filling

2 tablespoons olive oil

1½ pounds ground beef (85% lean)

1 small yellow onion, chopped

1 red bell pepper, cut into ½-inch squares

3 garlic cloves, finely chopped

¾ cup ketchup

2 tablespoons light brown sugar

2 tablespoons Worcestershire sauce

1 tablespoon cider vinegar

½ teaspoon smoked paprika

1 teaspoon chili powder

1 tablespoon Dijon mustard

¼ teaspoon crushed red pepper flakes

1 teaspoon sriracha

1 teaspoon kosher salt

¼ teaspoon freshly ground black pepper

¼ cup finely chopped fresh parsley

Assembly

All-purpose flour, for rolling

1 16.3-ounce tube refrigerated extra-large biscuits (such as Pillsbury Grands, 8 count)

1 cup shredded sharp cheddar cheese

Egg wash: 1 large egg beaten with 1 teaspoon water

MAKES 8 PIES The old-fashioned sloppy joe in a bun is an easy, family-friendly kind of meal. The saucy mix of ground beef, bell peppers, and onions is the perfect combination of tangy, spicy, and smoky. And this special hand pie version uses refrigerated biscuit dough for a simple and quick assembly. Be sure the beef filling is completely cold—you can even make it a couple of days in advance—because cold filling holds together better than room-temperature meat. Then, you can make these in no time. Serve them with your favorite slaw—cook's choice!

1. **MAKE THE FILLING:** Heat the oil in a large saucepan over medium-high heat. Add the ground beef and cook, stirring occasionally to break up the meat with the side of the spoon, until browned, 8 to 10 minutes. Pour off all but 2 tablespoons of the fat, leaving the beef in the saucepan.

2. Add the onion, bell pepper, and garlic and cook, stirring often, until the vegetables soften, about 3 to 5 minutes. Add the ketchup, ½ cup water, brown sugar, Worcestershire sauce, vinegar, smoked paprika, chili powder, mustard, pepper flakes, sriracha, salt, and black pepper and stir well. Bring to a simmer. Reduce the heat to low and simmer until thickened, about 15 minutes.

3. Stir in the parsley. Remove from the heat. Cool completely. (For best results, let the filling cool to room temperature, then transfer to a covered container and refrigerate until completely chilled, at least 2 hours or up to 3 days.)

4. **ASSEMBLE THE HAND PIES:** Preheat the oven to 400°F.

5. On a lightly floured work surface, roll out a biscuit into a 7-inch round. Place about ⅓ cup of the cold filling and 2 tablespoons cheddar in the bottom half of the round, leaving a ½-inch border. Fold the round in half and press the seam closed with the tines of a fork. Transfer to an ungreased half-sheet pan. Repeat with the remaining filling and biscuits. Brush the tops with the egg wash.

6. Bake until golden brown, 12 to 14 minutes. Serve hot.

Dessert, of Course!

I credit (or curse) my father for my ferocious sweet tooth. When we were younger, my two sisters, MaryAnn and Theresa, and I would go into the kitchen on a Sunday afternoon and have a dessert competition. Dad would name three things (say, a fruit pie, brownies, or an ice cream sundae), and we would each make a recipe. Dad was the judge in our junior "bake-off," so of course he had to try all three. Suffice it to say, I still take my sweets very seriously. Mom also instilled the love of baking for family and friends in me, with her daily dessert surprise, and I also always have something sweet tucked away in the kitchen.

There are three basic dessert categories that I go back to again and again. First, I want to share my favorite cookies with you. They range from Boozy Irish Cream Brownies (page 240) to no-bake "Chocolate Chips" (page 246). Your cookie jar will never be empty. I also have a few easy cakes that make many servings with very little effort. Try the Peach Olive Oil Cake (page 257) and the Pear (or Apple) Ginger Cakes (page 254) the next time your sweet tooth needs some love. And then I have some cool and creamy desserts that are perfect for our steamy New England summers. I guarantee that the Creamy Lemon Pie on page 261 will cool you down in a hurry.

Boozy Irish Cream Brownies

Brownies

Cooking spray

1 cup all-purpose flour

1/3 cup plus 1 tablespoon cocoa powder

1/2 teaspoon kosher salt

1 stick (4 ounces) unsalted butter, cut into tablespoons

1 1/2 cups sugar

6 ounces bittersweet chocolate, coarsely chopped, or 1 cup semisweet chocolate chips

1/3 cup Irish cream liqueur, preferably Baileys

2 large eggs

2 teaspoons vanilla extract

Frosting

1/2 cup Irish cream liqueur, preferably Baileys

1/4 cup heavy cream

12 ounces semisweet chocolate chips

MAKES 9 BROWNIES My kryptonite has always been frosted chocolate brownies—like from the time I was a small girl. They make me weak in the knees, and my sister MaryAnn loves to tell of how I used to bake pans of them and hide them under my bed with zero intention of sharing them. Yeah, I'm that girl. These brownies are ridiculously delicious. They are dense and fudgy with a subtle hint of Irish cream, my favorite liqueur, in them. Frost them with a blanket of silky and boozy chocolate ganache and you, too, will feel faint in their presence. Of course, save them for adults-only parties.

1. **MAKE THE BROWNIES:** Preheat the oven to 350°F. Mist a 9-inch square baking pan with cooking spray. Line the bottom with parchment paper.

2. In a medium bowl, whisk together the flour, cocoa, and salt.

3. Melt the butter and sugar in a medium saucepan over medium heat, stirring constantly, just until the butter melts and the mixture starts to bubble. Remove from the heat. Add the chocolate and let stand until the chocolate softens, about 2 minutes. Whisk until smooth. Let stand to cool slightly, 3 to 5 minutes.

4. Whisk the liqueur into the chocolate mixture. One at a time, whisk in the eggs, and then the vanilla. Scrape into the flour mixture and stir just until smooth. Spread the batter in the prepared baking dish and smooth the top.

5. Bake until a wooden toothpick inserted into the center comes out mostly clean, about 30 minutes.

6. Let cool completely in the baking dish on a wire rack. Invert the brownie onto the wire rack and remove the parchment. Flip the brownie right-side up.

Continues

7. **MAKE THE FROSTING:** Heat the liqueur and cream in a medium saucepan over medium heat, stirring occasionally, just until small bubbles appear around the edges. Remove from the heat. Stir in the chips, being sure they are submerged. Let stand until the chips soften, 3 to 5 minutes. Whisk until smooth. (This is now called a ganache.) Transfer to a medium bowl. Let stand at room temperature until the ganache thickens to a pudding consistency, about 2 hours. You can also refrigerate the ganache, stirring often to incorporate the firm edges into the soft center, until it is cool and thickened but not firm, about 1 hour.

8. Using an electric mixer set at medium speed, beat the ganache just until it is light and fluffy—this may take just a few seconds or so. Do not overbeat, or it will separate.

9. Spread over the cooled brownie and refrigerate until the frosting is set, about 30 minutes. Cut into 9 brownies and serve. (The brownies can be wrapped tightly in plastic wrap and stored at room temperature for up to 3 days.)

Molasses Sandwich Cookies

Molasses Cookies

2 cups all-purpose flour

2 teaspoons baking soda

1¼ teaspoons ground ginger

1 teaspoon ground cinnamon

½ teaspoon ground cloves

½ teaspoon kosher salt

1 cup packed dark brown sugar

1 stick (4 ounces) unsalted butter, at room temperature

2 tablespoons vegetable or canola oil

⅓ cup molasses (not blackstrap)

1 large egg, at room temperature

½ cup raw (turbinado) sugar, as needed, for rolling

Vanilla Cream Filling

1½ sticks (6 ounces) unsalted butter, at room temperature

3 cups powdered sugar

3 tablespoons heavy cream

1½ teaspoons vanilla extract

Pinch of kosher salt

MAKES 15 SANDWICH COOKIES These soft and chewy molasses cookies are perfectly spiced and are the epitome of wintertime baking. I always considered them the little black dress of the holiday season—simple, elegant, timeless, and forever stylish. With their crackly sugared surfaces, slightly crisped edges, and chewy interiors, they are nostalgic and therefore total crowd-pleasers. And just when you think they couldn't get any better, they do! Here I smash them together with a thick schmear of vanilla cream filling to turn a basic cookie into one of the most delicious and decadent offerings of your holiday cookie tray. Be sure to allow a couple of hours for the cookie dough to chill before baking to keep them from spreading too much.

1. **MAKE THE MOLASSES COOKIES:** In a medium bowl, whisk together the flour, baking soda, ginger, cinnamon, cloves, and salt. (Or use a sifter if you have one—the ingredients should be well combined and the baking soda well crumbled.)

2. In a large bowl, with an electric mixer, beat the brown sugar and butter together on high speed, occasionally scraping down the sides, until light in texture and color, about 2 minutes. Beat in the oil, followed by the molasses and egg, mixing well so the egg is absorbed.

3. Using a wooden spoon, stir in the flour mixture until combined. Cover and refrigerate until chilled and firm, at least 2 hours or up to 1 day.

4. Position racks in the center and top third of the oven and preheat to 350°F. Line two half-sheet pans with parchment paper.

5. Using 1 tablespoon for each cookie, shape the chilled dough into 30 balls. Put the raw sugar in a small bowl. One at a time, roll a ball in the sugar to coat, and arrange the balls 2 inches apart on the prepared half-sheet pans. Using the heel of your hand or the bottom of a flat glass, slightly flatten each ball.

Continues

6. Bake for 6 minutes. Switch racks and rotate the pans front to back. Continue baking until the edges are lightly browned but the centers are set and soft, about 6 minutes more.

7. Let the cookies cool for about 5 minutes on the pans before transferring to wire racks to cool completely. Be sure to let the sheets cool before using to bake more batches.

8. **MAKE THE VANILLA CREAM FILLING:** In a large bowl with an electric mixer, beat the butter on high speed until smooth. Reduce the speed to low and gradually beat in the powdered sugar. Return to high speed and beat, occasionally scraping down the sides of the bowl with a rubber spatula, until smooth, about 1 minute. Add the cream, vanilla, and salt and continue beating until the filling is fluffy, about 2 minutes.

9. Using a heaping tablespoon of filling for each cookie, sandwich the flat sides of two cookies together. (The cookies can be refrigerated in an airtight container for up to 5 days. Serve at room temperature.)

"Chocolate Chips"

1½ pounds (4 cups) semisweet chocolate chips (see Notes)

2 tablespoons coconut or vegetable oil

1 13-ounce bag wavy potato chips or other salty (or sweet) ingredients (see Notes)

Flaky sea salt, such as Maldon

Toffee bits, crushed nuts, or sprinkles (optional), for sprinkling

Notes

- You can substitute any kind of chocolate chips for the semisweet ones: Milk chocolate, white chocolate, and bittersweet chips all work well.

- In place of the potato chips, try other salted snacks, such as pretzels, corn chips, popcorn, or nuts.

- You could also use Oreos or graham crackers for a sweet variation.

MAKES ABOUT 36 Is this even considered a recipe since it's so ridiculously simple? Not really sure, but what I am sure about is that these little pretties are positively addictive and are the perfect party snack with the best flavor profile of crunchy, salty, and sweet. You'll know how easy they were to make, but everyone will think you ordered them from a chocolate shop!

1. Combine the chocolate chips and oil in the top pot of a double boiler (or a heatproof medium bowl) over simmering water. Heat, stirring occasionally, until the mixture is melted and smooth, about 3 minutes, depending on the brand of chocolate chips and the heat from the steaming water. Remove the top pot of the double boiler (or bowl) from the pan but keep the water simmering in case you need it later to remelt the chocolate.

2. Sort through the potato chips to choose the best-looking whole chips (use leftovers in Junkyard Cookies on page 248).

3. Line two half-sheet pans with parchment paper. One at a time, dip the potato chips into the melted chocolate mixture, either with your fingers or with two forks. Partially coat each chip on both sides (as shown) and lift it out, letting the excess chocolate drip back into the pot (or bowl). Transfer to the prepared pan. Sprinkle with the flaky salt and the optional toppings, if using. If the chocolate mixture begins to set, return to the double boiler and let it melt again, stirring often. Let the chips stand until set, about 1 hour. The chips can be carefully transferred to two 1-gallon resealable plastic bags and refrigerated for up to 10 days.

Junkyard Cookies

2¼ cups all-purpose flour

½ cup old-fashioned rolled oats

1 teaspoon baking soda

1 teaspoon kosher salt

2 sticks (8 ounces) unsalted butter, at room temperature

¾ cup granulated sugar

¾ cup packed light brown sugar

2 large eggs, at room temperature

1¼ teaspoons vanilla extract

2 cups coarsely crushed sturdy potato chips (see Notes)

2 cups coarsely crushed pretzels (see Notes)

1 cup semisweet chocolate chips

1 cup butterscotch chips

1 cup chopped unsalted peanuts

½ cup toffee chips

MAKES ABOUT 30 COOKIES These guys, with their oatmeal cookie base, have everything you could possibly want in a cookie: They are thick, soft, sweet, salty, and crunchy and are made with a hodgepodge of treats. The add-ins are flexible and can be adjusted to suit your tastes, and they are a great excuse to clean out the random odds and ends in your baking cabinet and pantry. Basically anything you want to jam into the dough will work—white chocolate chips, any kind of nut, raisins, you get the idea. I devised this recipe because every one of my kids had a favorite drop cookie (chocolate or butterscotch chip, oatmeal-raisin, and so on), so I figured using them all in one dough would be diplomatic. It makes a lot of dough, so do what my daughter Marcelle does: Bake as many as you want and freeze the leftover balls of dough for another time.

1. In a bowl, whisk together the flour, oats, baking soda, and salt.

2. In a large bowl, with an electric mixer, beat the butter, granulated sugar, and brown sugar on high speed, occasionally scraping down the sides of the bowl with a rubber spatula, until light in color and texture, about 2 minutes. One at a time, beat in the eggs, beating well until each egg is absorbed into the butter mixture. Beat in the vanilla. Using a wooden spoon, stir in the flour mixture until combined.

3. In a medium bowl, mix together the potato chips, pretzels, chocolate chips, butterscotch chips, peanuts, and toffee chips. Add to the dough and stir to combine. Cover with plastic wrap and refrigerate until chilled, at least 1 hour or up to 1 day.

4. Position racks in the center and top third of the oven and preheat to 350°F. Line two half-sheet pans with parchment paper.

5. Using a ¼-cup ice cream scoop for each cookie, or a palmful of dough, shape the chilled dough into balls and arrange about 3 inches apart on the prepared half-sheet pans. (To freeze the balls for later baking, see Notes.) Do not crowd them, as these spread into big cookies. Using the heel of your hand or the bottom of a flat glass, slightly flatten each ball.

6. Bake for 6 minutes. Switch racks and rotate the pans front to back. Continue baking until the edges are lightly browned but the centers are set and soft, about 6 minutes more.

7. Let the cookies cool for about 5 minutes on the pans before transferring to wire racks to cool completely. Be sure to let the sheets cool before using to bake more batches. (The cookies can be stored in an airtight container for up to 4 days, or frozen for up to 3 months.)

Notes

• Thick, wavy potato chips designed for dipping are the best choice for these cookies. Thin chips won't retain their crunch in the dough.

• To crush the chips and pretzels, drop them into a 1-gallon resealable plastic bag, seal the bag, and smash them with a rolling pin or empty wine bottle. You want pieces that are about 1/4-inch-square, so be careful not to crush them into a fine dust.

• Chilling the dough for drop cookies like these before baking reduces spreading, which keeps them nice and plump. You can also freeze the dough so you can have fresh-baked cookies whenever the mood strikes you. To do this, just freeze the balls on a baking sheet until they are frozen hard, about 1 hour. Then, transfer them to a 1-gallon resealable freezer bag and freeze for up to 3 months. Bake the frozen balls in a preheated 350°F oven for about 15 minutes.

Strawberry-Oat Bars

Cooking spray

Filling

2 cups coarsely chopped hulled fresh strawberries

2 tablespoons all-purpose flour

1 12-ounce jar strawberry jam

Finely grated zest and juice of 1/2 lemon

Dough

2 cups old-fashioned rolled oats

1½ cups all-purpose flour

3/4 cup packed light brown sugar

1 teaspoon baking powder

1/2 teaspoon kosher salt

2 sticks (8 ounces) unsalted butter, melted and cooled

MAKES 20 BARS My Grandma Murphy was a tea drinker and had a wicked sweet tooth. Every afternoon she asked for her "cuppa," and we always knew that she had to have a "little something" to accompany it. Mom and I were usually the ones to oblige her and this is the exact type of homemade treat that she was happiest to get. This is a variation of the oat bar recipe that Mom always made. They are super versatile because you can make them with any combination of jam and berries that you want. I'm pretty darn confident that these bars could pass for breakfast (because, oats), but they're equally delicious as a lunchbox treat, cut up for a potluck or a picnic, or served warm with ice cream for dessert as a sort of cobbler moment.

1. Preheat the oven to 350°F. Coat a 9 × 13-inch baking pan with cooking spray. Line the bottom and two short sides of the pan with parchment paper, letting the excess parchment hang over the ends as handles.

2. **MAKE THE FILLING:** In a medium bowl, sprinkle the strawberries with the flour and mix well. Add the strawberry jam, lemon zest, and lemon juice and mix again.

3. **MAKE THE DOUGH:** In a large bowl, whisk together the oats, flour, brown sugar, baking powder, and salt. Add the melted butter and stir until combined. Set aside 1 cup of the mixture for the topping. Press the remaining dough firmly and evenly into the pan.

4. Bake for 10 minutes. Remove from the oven and spread the filling evenly over the crust. Sprinkle evenly with the reserved oat mixture. Return to the oven and bake until the topping is golden brown and the filling is bubbling, 20 to 25 minutes longer.

5. Transfer the pan to a wire rack to cool completely.

6. Run a knife around the sides of the pastry to loosen it from the pan. Lift up with the parchment handles to remove the pastry in one piece. Using a large knife, cut the pastry lengthwise into 4 strips and then crosswise into 5 rows to make 20 bars. (The bars can be stored in an airtight container, separating the layers with parchment or waxed paper, for up to 3 days.)

Chocolate Root Beer Cake

Root Beer Cake

Cooking spray

2 cups all-purpose flour

1¼ teaspoons baking soda

1 teaspoon kosher salt

2 cups high-quality root beer (not diet)

1 cup unsweetened cocoa powder (not Dutch-process)

1 stick (4 ounces) unsalted butter, cut up

1¼ cups granulated sugar

½ cup packed light brown sugar

2 teaspoons vanilla extract

2 large eggs

Ganache

⅓ cup heavy cream

¼ teaspoon instant espresso or coffee

½ cup (3 ounces) semisweet chocolate chips

MAKES 12 TO 16 SERVINGS The root beer in this cake is no joke. The soda pop enhances the chocolate flavor, similar to the pairing of coffee and chocolate. You'll have a moist, fudgy cake that is richer and more complex than your regular chocolate Bundt. One caveat—this does not taste strongly of root beer, but its rich flavor and moist crumb are irresistible. (And yes, you can use another "brown" soda, such as cola or Dr Pepper.) The chocolate icing is optional, and the cake is also great with a dusting of powdered sugar or cocoa. Long story short, you gotta make this cake.

1. **MAKE THE ROOT BEER CAKE:** Preheat the oven to 325°F. Mist a 12-cup nonstick fluted tube pan with cooking spray.

2. In a medium bowl, whisk together the flour, baking soda, and salt.

3. In a large saucepan, combine the root beer, cocoa, and butter. Heat over medium heat, whisking constantly, until the butter is melted and the mixture is smooth. Add the granulated sugar and brown sugar and whisk until dissolved. Remove from the heat and whisk in the vanilla. Let cool for 15 minutes.

4. One at a time, whisk the eggs into the root beer mixture in the saucepan, whisking well after each addition. In two or three additions, whisk the flour mixture into the saucepan, and whisk until smooth. Scrape into the prepared tube pan.

5. Bake until a wooden skewer inserted into the cake comes out clean, about 40 minutes.

6. Let cool for 20 minutes in the pan on a wire rack. Place another cooling rack on top and invert to unmold the cake onto the rack, then let cool completely.

7. **MAKE THE GANACHE:** Bring the cream and instant espresso to a simmer in a medium saucepan over medium heat, whisking to dissolve the coffee. Remove from the heat. Add the chips and let stand to soften the chips, about 3 minutes. Whisk until smooth.

8. Place the cake on a rack over a half-sheet pan. Drizzle the ganache on top of the cake. Refrigerate to set the ganache, about 20 minutes. Slice and serve. (The cake can be stored at room temperature, wrapped in plastic wrap, for up to 3 days.)

Pear (or Apple) Ginger Cakes

Cooking spray

2 cups all-purpose flour

1 cup whole wheat flour

2 teaspoons ground cinnamon

1½ teaspoons ground ginger

1 teaspoon ground nutmeg

1 teaspoon baking soda

½ teaspoon ground cloves

1 teaspoon kosher salt

1½ cups packed light brown sugar

½ cup olive oil

½ cup unsweetened applesauce

¼ cup honey, plus more for brushing

2 tablespoons finely chopped crystallized ginger

3 large eggs, at room temperature

2 teaspoons vanilla extract

3 ripe Comice or Anjou pears (see Note), peeled, cored, and chopped (about 2½ cups)

½ cup chopped pecans

Note

If you happen to have another piece or two of fruit, you can use them to decorate the loaves. Peel, cut in half lengthwise, core, and cut the fruit crosswise into slices ⅛ inch thick. Arrange the slices on top of the loaves before baking.

MAKES 2 LOAVES (6 TO 8 SERVINGS EACH) I always keep a large bowl of fruit on the dining room table so the kids can grab a snack as they come in and out. But inevitably, when the bowl runs low, there are always a few stragglers that end up looking sad and bruised and lonely. Never fear! When that happens, just peel and cut them up and plop them into this cake where no one cares anymore that they were the runts of the litter. This is also great with apples, but use apples that hold their shape after baking, such as Gala, Golden Delicious, or Fuji, and skip eating or sauce apples like Red Delicious or McIntosh. Note that this provides two loaves, making it a perfect cake for gift-giving.

1. Preheat the oven to 350°F. Coat two 8 × 4-inch loaf pans with cooking spray. Line the bottoms of the pans with parchment or waxed paper.

2. In a medium bowl, whisk together the all-purpose flour, whole wheat flour, cinnamon, ground ginger, nutmeg, baking soda, cloves, and salt.

3. In a large bowl, whisk together the brown sugar, oil, applesauce, honey, and crystallized ginger. Add the eggs and vanilla and whisk well to incorporate. Add the flour mixture to the egg mixture and stir well, just to combine. Fold in the pears and pecans. Scrape into the loaf pans and smooth the tops.

4. Bake until a wooden toothpick inserted in the centers of the loaves comes out almost clean, about 40 minutes.

5. Remove from the oven and brush some honey on top to give it a glaze. (The honey will melt and spread when it meets the hot cake.) Let cool completely in the pans on a wire rack.

VARIATION

Pear-Ginger Muffins: Line 12 jumbo or 24 standard muffin cups with paper liners and spray the liners with cooking spray. Divide the batter evenly among the cups. Bake until golden brown and a wooden toothpick inserted in the center of a muffin comes out almost clean, about 20 minutes. Serve warm or cooled to room temperature.

Peach Olive Oil Cake

Cooking spray

1½ cups all-purpose flour

2 teaspoons baking powder

¼ teaspoon kosher salt

¾ cup sugar

½ cup extra-virgin olive oil

¾ cup whole-milk Greek yogurt

3 large eggs

1 teaspoon vanilla extract

Finely grated zest of 1 lemon

2 peaches, cut into wedges, or 2 cups thawed frozen slices

⅓ cup peach jam, heated until spreadable

SERVES 8 This simple cake is my go-to dessert when I need to whip up something special for unexpected guests or a last-minute invite. It is unfussy, not overly sweet (thanks to lemon zest and yogurt), and has a wonderful fluffy texture. It is a positively perfect companion to a cup of coffee. While it is best with fresh summer peaches, frozen ones are good, too. I've also used other stone fruits like plums and nectarines, as well as berries, figs, pears, and apples.

1. Preheat the oven to 350°F. Coat a 9-inch springform pan with cooking spray.

2. In a small bowl, whisk together the flour, baking powder, and salt.

3. In a large bowl with an electric mixer, beat the sugar and oil on high speed until the mixture is very pale, about 2 minutes. Add the yogurt, eggs, vanilla, and lemon zest and beat until combined. Add the flour mixture and mix on low speed, scraping down the sides of the bowl as needed, just until combined. Scrape into the prepared pan and smooth the top. Arrange the peach slices on top of the cake.

4. Bake until the cake is golden brown and a wooden toothpick inserted in the center comes out clean, 40 to 45 minutes.

5. Transfer the cake to a wire rack. Brush the top of the cake with the warm peach jam. Let cool in the pan for at least 20 minutes. Remove the sides of the pan and serve warm or let cool completely.

Berry and Cream Cheese Galette with Pistachio Crust

1 disk Pistachio Dough for Sweet Galettes (recipe follows)

4 ounces cream cheese, at room temperature

⅓ cup plus 2 teaspoons granulated sugar

1 large egg yolk

4 cups fresh berries, such as blueberries, blackberries, or raspberries, in any combination

2 tablespoons cornstarch

Finely grated zest and juice of ½ lemon

All-purpose flour, for rolling the dough

Egg wash: 1 large egg beaten with 1 teaspoon water

Raw (turbinado) or granulated sugar, for sprinkling

Whipped cream or vanilla ice cream, for serving

Note

If you want to make six individual galettes, use the full recipe for the dough and portion into six even rounds, about 4 inches in diameter.

SERVES 6 TO 8 A free-form galette is the fruit pie's unintimidating, free-spirited little sister, who is totally down for rustic ragged edges and overall low-maintenance lopsidedness. And I love her for it. She's as delicious and impressive as pie, but half the work and completely devoid of any of the anxiety-inducing crimping, trimming, and weaving that makes me keep a respectable distance from the pie business. Hey, we all have our strengths, right? This recipe is super versatile because you can use any type of berry.

1. Make the dough and chill as directed.

2. In a small bowl, combine the cream cheese, 2 teaspoons of the granulated sugar, and the yolk and mash with a silicone or rubber spatula until smooth and combined.

3. In a medium bowl, mix the berries, remaining ⅓ cup granulated sugar, the cornstarch, lemon zest, and lemon juice.

4. Preheat the oven to 350°F. Line a half-sheet pan with parchment paper.

5. On a lightly floured work surface, roll out the dough into a 12-inch round. Transfer to the prepared pan. Spread the cream cheese mixture over the round, leaving a 2-inch border, and scatter the coated berries on top. Fold the dough up where it meets the filling to partially cover the berries, pleating the dough as you go. Brush the dough with the egg wash and sprinkle the sugar over the dough. Refrigerate until chilled, 15 to 30 minutes.

6. Bake until the pastry is golden brown and the berry juices are bubbling, 40 to 45 minutes.

7. Let cool on the pan until warm (or cool to room temperature). Transfer the galette to a serving platter. Cut into wedges and serve with the whipped cream.

Continues

PISTACHIO DOUGH FOR SWEET GALETTES

Makes enough for two 8-inch galettes

½ cup pistachios

2½ cups all-purpose flour, plus more for rolling

1 teaspoon sugar

1 teaspoon kosher salt

2 sticks (8 ounces) cold unsalted butter, cut into ½-inch pieces

½ cup ice water

I love sweet galettes so much that when I make this dough, I make enough so I can freeze half for another galette in the future.

1. Pulse the pistachios in a food processor until they are finely chopped. Add the flour, sugar, and salt and pulse to combine. Scatter the butter on top and pulse until the mixture looks like coarse crumbs with some pea-sized chunks of butter. With the machine running, pour the ice water through the feed tube and stop the machine as soon as the dough clumps together.

2. Turn out the dough onto a lightly floured work surface and press into a ball. Cut in half, shape each portion into a thick disk, and wrap each in plastic wrap. Refrigerate until chilled, 30 minutes to 1 hour. (Or if using the dough later, pop in the freezer. The dough can be frozen for up to 3 months. Thaw overnight in the refrigerator. Let stand at room temperature for about 20 minutes before rolling out.)

Creamy Lemon Pie

Crust

1½ cups coarsely crushed graham cracker crumbs (about 11 crackers)

¼ cup sugar

⅛ teaspoon kosher salt

1 stick (4 ounces) unsalted butter, melted

Filling

2 14-ounce cans sweetened condensed milk

4 large egg yolks

Finely grated zest of 1 lemon

¾ cup fresh lemon juice

⅛ teaspoon kosher salt

Whipped Cream

2 cups heavy cream

¼ cup sugar

Note

If your pie pan is a standard pan, which isn't 1½ inches deep, there will be leftover filling and a thicker crumb crust.

SERVES 8 Funny story: My husband and I have been married more than thirty years, and I thought I had a handle on his likes and dislikes, especially with food. I told everyone that key lime was his favorite pie. Then, some time ago, he blurted out, "Di, I have to tell you that key lime pie is not my favorite." Once I picked my jaw up off the floor, I asked him why he never told me all these years. He said, "I just didn't want to contradict you in public," which is really very sweet. Now when he wants pie, I make this super-simple lemon pie with a tall pillow of whipped cream . . . although I am not convinced that he prefers it to key lime after all.

1. **MAKE THE CRUST:** Preheat the oven to 325°F.

2. In a food processor, combine the graham crackers, sugar, and salt and process until you have fine crumbs. Add the melted butter and pulse until the mixture looks like wet sand. Transfer to a 9½-inch pie dish 1½ inches deep (see Note). Using the palm of your hand or the bottom of a 1-cup measuring cup, press the crumb mixture firmly and evenly into the pie dish.

3. Bake until the pie crust smells toasty and is beginning to brown on the edges, 10 to 15 minutes. Transfer to a wire rack and let cool slightly. Leave the oven on.

4. **MAKE THE FILLING:** In a large bowl, whisk together the condensed milk and yolks until combined. Add the lemon zest, lemon juice, and salt and whisk until smooth. Pour into the warm crust.

5. Return to the oven and bake until the edges of the filling are set when the pie is jiggled, but the very center moves as a mass, about 20 minutes.

6. Transfer to the rack and let cool for about 15 minutes. Cover with plastic wrap and refrigerate until chilled, at least 3 hours or overnight.

7. **MAKE THE WHIPPED CREAM:** In a stand mixer fitted with the whisk, whip the cream and sugar on high speed until it forms stiff peaks. Spread the whipped cream over the chilled pie. Slice and serve.

Snickers Pie

Crust

Softened butter, for the pie plate

22 Oreo cookies (the original vanilla-filled chocolate cookies)

5 tablespoons unsalted butter, melted

Filling

1 cup (6 ounces) semisweet chocolate chips

1½ cups marshmallow creme, such as Marshmallow Fluff

4 ounces cream cheese, at room temperature

½ cup creamy peanut butter

½ cup heavy cream

2 tablespoons unsalted butter, at room temperature

7 ounces (about 26) soft caramels, unwrapped

½ cup chopped salted or unsalted roasted peanuts

Chocolate shavings (optional; see Note), for topping

SERVES 8 TO 10 Ever since my daughter Mary was a little girl, she would hide Snickers bars in her bedroom and I'd find wrappers shoved into every corner of the house. Her obsession with this candy motivated me to come up with a dessert that would please her just as much as those candy bars did. So, here is a pie of pure decadence, filled with caramel, peanuts, chocolate, and a creamy, dreamy peanut butter filling. It's heaped into a chocolate cookie crumb crust. This is an absolutely melt-in-your-mouth dessert.

1. **MAKE THE CRUST:** Preheat the oven to 350°F. Lightly butter a 9-inch pie plate.

2. In a food processor, pulse the Oreos, with their filling, until they form fine crumbs. Drizzle the melted butter over the crumbs and pulse to combine. Transfer to the pie plate and, using the bottom of a 1-cup measuring cup or your hands, press the crumbs firmly and evenly into the bottom and sides of the plate.

3. Bake until the crust is set, about 10 minutes. Remove the crust from the oven.

4. **MAKE THE FILLING:** Immediately scatter the chocolate chips over the bottom of the hot crust. Let stand to soften the chips, about 5 minutes. Using a small offset spatula or the back of a spoon, spread the chocolate on the bottom of the crust. Refrigerate until the chocolate is set, about 30 minutes.

5. Meanwhile, in a medium bowl with an electric mixer, beat together the marshmallow creme, cream cheese, peanut butter, heavy cream, and butter on high speed, scraping down the sides of the bowl as needed, until light and fluffy, about 2 minutes. Set aside.

6. Melt the caramels with ¼ cup water in a medium saucepan over medium heat, stirring occasionally, until melted and smooth, about 10 minutes.

7. Beat about 2 tablespoons of the caramel into the marshmallow mixture. Allow the remaining caramel to cool slightly, then spread it evenly over the chocolate in the crust and sprinkle with the peanuts. Return to the refrigerator and chill until the caramel is set, about 10 minutes.

8. Spread the marshmallow mixture over the peanuts. Refrigerate, uncovered, until the filling is chilled and set, at least 4 hours or preferably overnight. Top with the chocolate shavings, if desired. Slice and serve chilled.

Note

While you can sometimes find chocolate shavings sold in bakery supply shops, it is super easy to make your own at home. Start with a hunk of semisweet chocolate weighing at least 4 ounces. Microwave the chocolate at 50% power for about 15 seconds. The idea is to slightly warm the chocolate, not melt it. It needs to be a little warmer than room temperature. Working over a sheet of waxed paper, use a vegetable peeler to shave curls from the chocolate. If the chocolate shatters instead of making curls, microwave the chocolate for another 10 to 15 seconds. Refrigerate the shavings until ready to use. Shake the shavings from the waxed paper over the pie. If you touch them with your fingers, they could melt.

Affogato with Chocolate Ganache

Ganache

½ cup heavy cream

4 ounces high-quality bittersweet chocolate (60% to 70% cacao), coarsely chopped

Whipped Cream

1 cup heavy cream

1 tablespoon powdered sugar

1 teaspoon vanilla extract

Assembly

1 quart vanilla gelato

8 tablespoons espresso, at room temperature (see Note)

8 tablespoons nut liqueur, such as amaretto or Frangelico

About ⅓ cup coarsely crushed amaretti cookies or small biscotti

Note

Home-kitchen espresso machines are common these days, so getting the brewed espresso doesn't require a trip to a local café. You can go Old World, like Grandma did, by making the espresso with a metal stovetop moka pot. Or brew up a pot of dark roast coffee in a drip coffee maker.

SERVES 4 *Affogato* means "drowned" in Italian, and that's exactly what this dessert is: ice cream drowned in cooled espresso. I have been loving it since I was a small child. And while I love the simplicity of this original version, my rendition is a bit more jacked up with the addition of whipped cream, chocolate ganache, and an optional shot of liqueur. It's a decadent dessert and an after-dinner drink all rolled into one. Each bite delivers a wonderful burst of rich creaminess with an occasional bit of crunch from cookie crumbs, taking a simple dessert and making it extraordinary.

1. **MAKE THE GANACHE:** Heat the cream in a small saucepan over medium heat until bubbles appear around the edge. Remove from the heat and add the chocolate, stirring to be sure the chocolate is submerged. Let stand until the chocolate softens, about 2 minutes. Whisk until smooth. Let cool for 15 to 30 minutes. (The ganache must be pourable, so don't let it cool too long or it will set up. Reheat gently, if needed.)

2. **MAKE THE WHIPPED CREAM:** In a chilled bowl with an electric mixer (with chilled beaters), beat the cream, powdered sugar, and vanilla on high speed until soft peaks form. Refrigerate until ready to serve.

3. **TO ASSEMBLE:** For each serving, add 2 or 3 scoops of gelato to a small glass bowl. (I often do this beforehand and keep the ice cream frozen in the bowls until ready to serve.) Pour 2 tablespoons espresso and 2 tablespoons liqueur over the ice cream, then top each with an equal amount of ganache. Top each with a dollop of whipped cream and a generous sprinkling of cookie crumbs. Serve immediately.

Pots de Crème

6 large egg yolks

1/3 cup granulated sugar

2 cups whole milk

1 cup heavy cream

Pinch of kosher salt

10 ounces bittersweet chocolate chips (around 60% cacao, such as Ghirardelli)

1/2 teaspoon instant espresso powder

Whipped Cream

1/2 cup heavy cream

1 tablespoon powdered sugar

SERVES 6 When my siblings and I were young, my grandmother would often serve us desserts in her demitasse espresso cups, the perfect size for our tiny hands. She usually just filled the little cups with Jell-O, sherbet, or pudding, but I relive the wonderful memory with these pots de crème. Rich, silky smooth, and decadent, they are fancy enough to serve at a dinner party yet simple enough for a midweek treat. I like to get a deeper flavor with bittersweet chocolate chips instead of the more common semisweet. The chips are convenient, but you can also chop up bittersweet chocolate bars. Make these ahead of time and top with whipped cream just before serving.

1. In a heavy-bottomed medium saucepan, whisk together the yolks and granulated sugar until thickened. Gradually whisk in the milk, cream, and salt. Cook over medium heat, stirring constantly with a wooden spoon, being sure to reach into the corners of the saucepan, until the mixture is steaming, almost simmering, and thick enough to coat the spoon (it will read 185°F on an instant-read thermometer), 10 to 12 minutes. If you draw your finger down the custard on the spoon, it will cut a swath. Do not allow the mixture to boil! Remove from the heat.

2. Add the chocolate chips and espresso powder to the saucepan and gently stir them in. Let stand until the chips soften more, about 3 minutes. Using a clean whisk, whisk well until the mixture is silky smooth. Strain through a wire-mesh sieve set over a large measuring cup with a spout.

3. Dividing equally, pour the mixture into six coffee cups or ramekins. Cover each with plastic wrap. Refrigerate until chilled and set, at least 4 hours or preferably overnight.

4. **MAKE THE WHIPPED CREAM:** In a bowl with an electric mixer (or using a whisk), whip the cream with the powdered sugar on high speed until the cream forms soft peaks.

5. Top each dessert with a dollop of whipped cream and serve chilled.

Acknowledgments

I could not have arrived at this point without the people who helped make things happen.

First and foremost, thank you to Esther Newberg, literary agent extraordinaire. She slid into my DMs and asked me if I had ever thought about writing a cookbook. I had, and many people had approached me before she did, but it never felt right. I didn't know what I was waiting for until I spoke with Esther on the phone one day for two hours, after which I knew exactly what I had been waiting for: It was Esther. Esther, you and Kristyn Keene Benton have made this entire process enjoyable. Thank you for believing in me.

Thank you to my editor, Doris Cooper. Many people could have acquired my book, but you were the one who took a chance on me, and, in the process, taught me so much. I didn't know what I didn't know, and there is no manual for writing your first book, but I didn't need one because I had you. I felt supported and validated every step of the way, and when I felt even the slightest bit of self-doubt, you were my constant cheerleader. Thank you also to Katie McClimon for keeping me organized and jumping on a Zoom call at the drop of a dime to explain something to me, and to Laura Palese for designing a book that felt exactly like me. Thank you to the rest of the Simon Element team: Richard Rhorer, Jessica Preeg, Elizabeth Breeden, Jen Wang, and Laura Jarrett.

Rick Rodgers, with his incredible experience and vast knowledge about writing cookbooks, made writing one less intimidating. Your wealth of information and willingness to share it with me were invaluable when it came to my completing this enormous task. Thank you for caring as much as you did. I could not have done this without you.

To Ina Garten, my first girl crush, I simply adore you. From the time your first cookbook came out in 1999 and with every subsequent publication, you have been my constant source of inspiration. You were the one who first made me think "Maybe I could, too, one day." Thank you for that.

Photographing a cookbook is no joke. Thank you to the amazing group of creative people who brought their talent and expertise to this book's photography. I witnessed the thought, time, patience, attention to detail, and flexibility that went into every single shot and my gratitude runneth over for the team: Dane Tashima is the most incredible photographer, and he, along with Jane Gaspar and Jack Koto, his digital technicians, made the shoots smooth. It was an absolute joy to watch them do their thing. I knew from minute one that I was in expert hands. Suzanne Lenzer and Liza Jernow are exceptional food stylists, as are assistants Ken Rath and Jahqyad Austin. I didn't think I could manage my control-freak tendencies when it came to making the food, but I quickly learned to trust your vision and impeccable eyes. Christina Wressel and her assistant Seamus Crighton are phenomenal prop stylists. It was so cool to watch them approach each shot with the exact items we needed to tell my story. They are a joy to be around, and I appreciate them more than they know.

Thank you to Judy Sieber from the wonderful Emily Joubert in California and to J.Crew for gifting and loaning me the beautiful serving pieces, linens, and wardrobe.

To Christina Minardi, the best boss I ever had. Thank you for everything.

Thank you to my followers who encouraged me to use my voice and write a book—and for finding me and sticking around. My foray into social media was a happy accident, and you showed up for me consistently and gave me the confidence to believe that a book was the next natural step for me. You inspire me every day and incentivize me to share what I love to do.

To my five siblings, Andrew, Mary Ann, Michael, Theresa, and Thomas, thank you for being the best hype team a girl could ever hope to have. Your never-ending support system means the world to me. I am so lucky to have you in my corner.

My grandmother Lucrezia Lagravinese Montelli's pure love for food and family was my first lesson in the concept that Food Is Love. I am forever grateful to her for that.

To my mom and dad, who were *so* proud of me when I told them I was writing a book. I don't think they ever fully understood what I did for a living, but whatever I did throughout my life, I had the two biggest cheerleaders in my corner. I won the parent lottery. Dad, I know, is now watching me from above with a big smile.

To my husband, John, thank you for being my very best support system. John and I have been happily married for more than three decades, despite the fact that I still call him my boyfriend. You can say that you married the best guy around, but when you've been married as long as we have, you know you chose well. I got a good one. 143, babe.

And, finally, to my six biggest fans: Marcelle, Mary Grace, Patrick, Frances, John Paul, and Luke, you are the reason why I am where I am today. When my Instagram account was hacked back in 2019, I was ready to throw in the towel. But all six of you said to me, "Mom, you *can't* quit. You love teaching and sharing food." And you know what? You were absolutely right. So, despite the fact that I didn't have the heart to begin again, I thought about what kind of message that would send to my children. I didn't want them to see that I quit when the going got tough, so I persevered, started again, and showed that you never give up. Thank you, kids, for inspiring me with that valuable lesson, and thank you for being my main reasons for showing up daily. I am so blessed to be your Mama.

Index

NOTE: Page numbers in *italics* indicate photos of recipes or recipe preparation.